LEBANESE
COOKBOOK

LEBANESE COOKBOOK

Dawn, Elaine and Selwa Anthony

Lansdowne
Sydney Auckland London New York

Baked Stuffed Kibbi Loaf (page 57) surrounded by Hoummus b'Tahini (page 34),
Kibbi Nayye (page 56) Tabbouleh (page 88) and Lebanese Bread (page 31).

ACKNOWLEDGEMENTS

We express our gratitude to Mrs Freda Melick, Mrs Katrine McGuire and Mrs Theresa Alam, who over the past fifty years have set an example in Australia of Lebanese cooking at its best. Together with our mother, they provided the memories of delectable Lebanese food which were the inspiration for this book.

We thank, also, the twenty-five friends and relatives who enthusiastically tested the recipes and offered constructive criticism and advice.

We are deeply indebted to Josephine and Nagi Hayek, Mr Naseeb Gaha, Mrs Nagwa Nasr, Mrs Lily Asly, Mrs Toni Gaha, Mrs Yvette Clarke and the staff of Lebanese Import/Export, Sydney, for their help with research and translation, to Mrs Barbara Armstrong for her competent secretarial assistance, and to our Publishers for providing the competent, vital assistance of editor Helen Frazer, the artistry of universally acclaimed photographer Reg Morrison and the expert design talents of Bruno Grasswill — their combined efforts have turned a cookbook into a work of art.

Last, but not least, we thank our mother, Mrs Josephine Anthony, who prepared the food for photography and without whose assistance this book could not have been written.

*Dedicated to the expert —
Our Mother*

> Crockery, glassware and cooking utensils for photography were supplied courtesy of Village Living, Avalon, NSW, in conjunction with Danfield Pty Ltd, Sydney, NSW.

NOTE:
The anglicised spellings of Arabic words used in this book have been selected strictly to facilitate easy pronunciation.

Published by Lansdowne Press, Sydney
a division of RPLA Pty Limited
176 South Creek Road, Dee Why West, N.S.W., Australia, 2099.
First published 1978
6th Impression 1986
© Copyright RPLA Pty Limited 1978.
Produced in Australia by the Publisher
Typeset in Australia by G.T. Setters Pty. Ltd.
Printed in Hong Kong by South China Printing Co.

National Library of Australia Cataloguing-in-Publication Data

Anthony, Dawn.
  Lebanese cookbook.

  First published: Sydney: Ure Smith, 1978.
  Includes index.
  ISBN 0 7018 1753 4.

  1. Cookery, Lebanese. I Anthony, Elaine.
  II. Anthony, Selwa. III. Title.

641 59562

CONTENTS

INTRODUCTION

Lebanese cuisine has evolved from a background of Arab culture in a country which has been the trading link between East and West for thousands of years. It is a country which produces ample good, natural food and where people enjoy practising the grace of Arab hospitality. This hospitality requires an abundant table to be set at all times and necessitates a variety of food always being on hand to offer the unexpected guest.

Lebanese cuisine will delight the gourmet, for it is produced by a people who love good food, and satisfy the health enthusiast, because much use is made of grain, cheese, yoghurt, and fresh and dried fruits and vegetables. Even the vegetarian can find many tasty dishes within its scope — meat-free (vegetarian) recipes are marked with the symbol ⓥ for easy identification, and those that are both meat-free and dairy-free (lenten) also carry the symbol ⓛ.

All Lebanese recipes are extremely economical. With imaginative use of herbs, spices, grain and vegetables, meat goes a long way and even the simplest ingredients produce a tasty meal.

Lebanese cooking has been enjoyed for many years by travellers visiting the country, but only recently have Lebanese restaurants been established in any great number in Western countries. This food is now becoming very popular and a curiosity has been aroused about its origin.

To satisfy this curiosity we have included a little of the country's background and a description of the customs and manner of eating. We hope that this will help you to enjoy a truly Lebanese meal.

The recipes in this book have been handed down from mother to daughter for generations. We invite you to try them and wish you *Suhtain,* which means "enjoy this food in good health".

Dawn, Elaine and Selwa Anthony

A platter of Stuffed Grape Vine Leaves (page 78).

BRIEF GUIDE TO LEBANON

Lebanon—the biblical land of the "Song of Songs" and the homeland of the ancient Phoenicians—is one of the smallest and most fascinating countries in the world. Into its small area is packed a wealth of natural beauty and enormous human, historical and archaeological interest.

Measuring only 210 km (130 miles) in length and 75 km (46 miles) in width, it has a population of three million and is situated along the east coast of the Mediterranean between Syria and Israel. Its tiny coastline is dotted with the ancient ports of Tyre, Sidon, Byblos, Tripoli and Beirut.

One third of the total land mass is made up of mountains, which ascend suddenly in places to a height of 2450 metres (8000 feet) and are divided from north to south by the lush Bekaa Valley. On the steep mountain slopes, terraced villages perch precariously amid countless mountain springs and waterfalls.

The sheer sudden height of the mountains becomes obvious when you realise that it is possible, at certain times of the year, to swim in the warm Mediterranean waters at the foot of the mountains and one hour later, after motoring to the top, ski down the snowy slopes.

The Lebanese landscape varies from barren, rocky terrain to fertile valleys and plains.

Much of the countryside is covered in cypress, willow, poplar, oak and pine trees, and in places the remains of famous cedar forests are still evident. There are many olive groves and banana plantations, and countless thriving orchards which produce an abundance of citrus fruits, apricots, peaches, figs and pomegranates.

From December through to the northern spring, wildflowers of every colour begin to bloom. Among these are narcissus, iris, crocus, anemone, hibiscus, tulips and cyclamen. In the mountains flowers seem to grow everywhere, even in the stone walls of ancient ruins.

This picturesque country has been called the "Land of the Poets". For thousands of years it has inspired men to sing its praises, among them the great Lebanese poet and philosopher, Khalil Gibran.

Today Lebanon is a country of contrasts and diversities.

Beirut, the capital, is a sophisticated city bursting with luxury products, first class hotels, elegant women and fast cars. It has also, regrettably, been the scene of complex political conflicts.

The ancient Temple of Bacchus, Baalbeck.

National Council of Tourism, Lebanon/Fattal

13

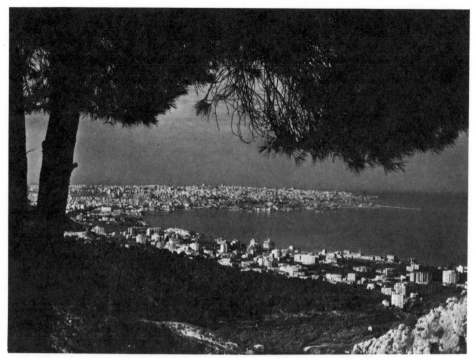

A panoramic view of Beirut. National Council of Tourism, Lebanon/Varoujan

These trappings of the modern world stand alongside old souks (market places) and ancient ruins.

In the villages people cling to old traditions. They live in simple, stone dwellings and retain a spontaneous outlook on life.

Everywhere you go, you come in contact with the past.

Ancient ruins blending into the landscape form a typical characteristic of the country. Archaeological discoveries include Babylonian, Egyptian, Roman, Greek, Byzantine and Arab constructions. Many Roman temples have been transformed into mosques or Byzantine churches and numerous village houses have been built with the debris of ancient monuments.

In the vast complex of the Roman ruins at Baalbeck are the temple of Bacchus, built around 150 AD and much larger than the Parthenon in Greece, and the temple of Heliopolitan Jupiter, the largest and most sumptuous in Roman antiquity. In ancient times this area was called the "granary of the Roman Empire".

The country is also dotted with churches, mosques, convents and monasteries. In the Christian sections, statues to the Virgin and lamp-lit altars are seen along the roadside.

The Lebanese are basically very religious, either Christian, Moslem or Druze. Even those who profess atheism adhere to religious customs.

They are also highly educated. As well as many religious schools there are over 1000 state schools and four universities.

Their heritage is one of academic, trade and cultural achievement.

Commencing 3000 years ago with the Phoenicians, the Lebanese

Famous cedars of Lebanon. National Council of Tourism, Lebanon/Yetenekian

were the merchant traders of the ancient world. The phonetic alphabet was developed here, and Phoenician travellers were the first to use the Polar Star for navigation. An interesting note is the flourishing trade they set up in a rare purple dye extracted from shellfish, which became known as Tyrian Purple. Only wealthy and famous people were permitted to wear this colour, so it became the status symbol of the day. Even now we hear the cliché "born to the purple".

The Arabs' left the deepest mark on Lebanese culture and from them the Lebanese took their language. Other early influences came from the Crusaders and the Turks. Modern Western influence arrived when Lebanon became a French Protectorate early in the twentieth century. French and American schools and universities were subsequently established, and today both French and English are spoken widely throughout the country.

The average Lebanese is extremely individualistic. He likes to "show off" but has a great sense of dignity and honour. He is always willing to be of assistance and is extremely hospitable.

From his Phoenician ancestors he has inherited an aptitude for business dealings and a fondness for travel. These two characteristics could help to account for the fact that the Lebanese are migratory people. It is estimated that there are as many Lebanese settlers abroad as those living in Lebanon. Areas of emigration include the United States, Canada, South America and Australia.

But whether at home or abroad, the Lebanese remain intensely proud of their culture and heritage.

THE LEBANESE CUISINE

It is with food that the Lebanese express their generosity and hospitality. The most casual caller is immediately offered a cup of coffee and even the unexpected visitor is pressed to stay on for an ample meal, which generally consists of a variety of dishes and can always be produced at extremely short notice.

The secret to mastering Lebanese cuisine lies in the preparation and organization of the menu and in the fact that Lebanese dishes store and reheat well.

The Lebanese cook always prepares several dishes in advance and stores the basic mixtures so that they can be combined with other food items to quickly make a full meal. Every household has a constant stock of pickles, olives, cheese, yoghurt, nuts, grain, herbs and spices.

Nearly every part of the raw product is utilized. In fact there is so little wastage that a small selection of raw food is sufficient to create a large variety of substantial dishes.

For example, five substantial meals for four people or an impressive spread for approximately ten people can be made with a large leg of mutton, ten tomatoes, ten zucchini, crushed wheat, rice, a few eggs, nuts, spices and herbs. To do this, the leg of mutton is boned and a broth made with the bones. The lean part of the meat is then minced and mixed with crushed wheat to make two varieties of *kibbi*, the national dish. The remainder of the meat is chopped and ground. Half of it is mixed with nuts and used as a filling for the tomatoes. The remaining meat, mixed with rice, is used to stuff scooped out zucchini. And the scooped out pulp of the zucchini, combined with eggs, makes tasty fritters. These dishes are then served as required, with rice or Bur'ghul Pilaf and the usual accompaniments of yoghurt, salad vegetables, bread and olives. The cook always endeavours to present food with a flavour that appeals to most palates and does not require additional seasoning at the table. Spices, herbs and natural flavourings are an integral part of most recipes, but as a rule they are not used overpoweringly.

The most widely used spices are nutmeg, cinnamon, cloves, various peppers, coriander, cumin, aniseed and gum arabic. Popular herbs are mint, parsley, sesame seeds, thyme, marjoram and sïm'meh. Flavourings include garlic, onions, lemons, olive oil, ghee, tomatoes, pine nuts, almonds, rosewater and orange blossom water.

The main meal in Lebanon is usually served in the evening, but on weekends and public holidays it may be eaten at midday. A main meal is always served when guests are present, whatever time of the day.

At the beginning of the main meal *mezza* (hors d'oeuvres) are served with drinks.

Mezza consists of a large variety of nuts, pickles, cheese and other foods, displayed in small dishes from which it is picked up with the fingers.

Mezza is an important part of Lebanese social life. It is a leisurely, relaxing period in which eating and drinking is accompanied by congenial conversation or a game of *torlie* (backgammon).

As the time taken up for mezza can extend to three hours or more, the main course will often be served at a very late hour. Sometimes, particularly during holidays or in restaurants, an elaborate mezza will take the place of a full meal.

Alcoholic beverages are never served without the accompaniment of at least a few mezza dishes. The main alcoholic beverage is *arack*, a grape extract flavoured with aniseed. Various wines, spirits and beers are also popular.

Traditionally only water is served with the main course, confining alcoholic drinks to the pre-dinner mezza period. However, today arack, wine or beer is often poured at the table or after a meal.

At least three dishes are served for the main course of the main meal. On important occasions, such as when guests are present or during a celebration, many more dishes are presented.

The main course usually consists of a meat, a cooked vegetable. and a grain dish, together with the usual accompaniments of yoghurt, salad, bread and olives. The food is placed on serving platters or in bowls on the centre of the table, and those at the table serve themselves, taking small portions of each variety of food or choosing larger portions of one or two dishes only.

At the completion of the main course, fresh or dried fruits are placed in the centre of the table and coffee is served, sometimes accompanied with sweet pastries or puddings.

Lebanese coffee is the strong Turkish variety with a thick sediment. It is served often and, like mezza, is an important part of the Lebanese way of life.

Visitors are always offered a cup of coffee, no matter what time of day or night, but a second cup is not offered at the same serving.

The average person probably drinks from 6-10 cups of coffee each day. These cups are tiny (smaller than demitasse) and the sediment is left in the bottom, so the daily coffee consumption does not amount to more than that in Western countries.

Traditionally, sweet coffee is served during festive times and bitter coffee is made for sad occasions.

Breakfast always includes coffee, bread and some of the following foods: black olives, cheese, *zaatar* (a herb mixture), eggs, fresh or dried fruit and jam.

A light meal is generally a bowl of soup or a cooked vegetable or grain dish, with accompaniments such as cheese, olives, salad vegetables and yoghurt. Sandwiches made from Lebanese bread are also very popular.

The following menus are examples of a typical Lebanese diet.

BREAKFAST

CREAM CHEESE
ZAATAR MIXTURE

Black Olives — Bread

Coffee
Fresh Fruit

LUNCH

DRIED BEANS WITH ONIONS
or
GREEN BEANS IN OIL

Spring Onions — Radish — Bread

Fresh Fruit

BREAKFAST

EGGS FRIED IN OLIVE OIL
ZAATAR MIXTURE

Black Olives — Bread

Coffee
Jams

LUNCH

COLD BAKED KIBBI IN OIL

Salad — Yoghurt — Olives —
Pickles — Bread

Rice Pudding

BREAKFAST

WHITE CHEESE

Black Olives — Bread

Coffee
Dried Fruits

LUNCH

BEAN AND GRAIN SOUP
or
BUR'GHUL AND LENTIL SOUP

Raw Onions — Radish — Olives

Dried Fruit

LUNCH

KIBBI BALLS IN YOGHURT

Bread — Olives — Cheese

Jams

LUNCH

LENTIL AND RICE PILAF
FATTOUSH

Radish — Olives — Spring Onions

Fresh Fruit

DINNER

Mezza

A selection of hors d'oeuvres and drinks

Main Course

BAKED STUFFED KIBBI LOAF

STUFFED EGGPLANTS

GREEN BEAN STEW

RICE PILAF

Salad — Olives — Bread

Coffee

Dried Fruits and Jams

DINNER

Mezza

A selection of hors d'oeuvres and drinks

Main Course

CHICKEN AND RICE SOUP

BAKED KIBBI SHELLS

OKRA STEW

BUR'GHUL PILAF

Yoghurt — Olives — Salad — Bread

Coffee

Fresh Fruit

DINNER

Mezza

A selection of hors d'oeuvres and drinks

Main Course

BAKED PEPPERED FISH

SMALL FRIED FISH

SPICY RICE FOR FISH

TAHINI SAUCE

Fried Bread Pieces — Fried Cauliflower,
Eggplant and Potatoes — Salad — Olives

Coffee

Fresh Fruit

DINNER

Mezza

A selection of hors d'oeuvres and drinks

Main Course

KAFTA ON SKEWERS

LAHEM MISHWI

KIBBI NAYYE

GRAPE VINE LEAF ROLLS

HOUMMUS B'TAHINI

TABBOULEH

Olives — Bread

Coffee

Dried Fruits

Rice Pudding

DINNER

Mezza

A selection of hors d'oeuvres and drinks

Main Course

CHICKEN AND RICE SOUP

BAKED KIBBI SHELLS

OKRA STEW

BUR'GHUL PILAF

Yoghurt — Olives — Salad — Bread

Coffee

Fresh Fruit

Sweet Pastries

INGREDIENTS AND EQUIPMENT

Most of the ingredients and equipment used in the Lebanese kitchen will be familiar to the Western cook, however in some instances the food is prepared differently. The following list contains all the information you need to know about the basic ingredients and equipment used throughout this book. Directions for specific areas are contained in the relevant chapters.

BUR'GHUL:
Bur'ghul is a crushed wheat which has been boiled, dried in the sun and then ground. It can be obtained from health food stores and delicatessens under the names of "bur'ghul" or "Lebanese crushed wheat" — do **not** use ordinary cracked wheat. The quantities given in the recipes refer to the dried grain, however it will swell up when you wash and drain it.

DRIED BEANS (and DRIED PEAS):
Dried beans should always be soaked before cooking. The best way to do this is to soak them overnight in a large bowl with three times their amount of cold water and a pinch of bicarbonate of soda, however if you are in a hurry you can reduce the time by omitting the bicarbonate of soda and bringing the beans and water to the boil, boiling for 2 minutes, then turning off the heat and allowing to stand for one hour.

When you are ready to cook the beans, drain off the water in which they were soaked, replace it with 3 times their amount of fresh water and bring to the boil. Cover and simmer strongly, stirring occasionally, until the water is well reduced — approx 20-30 minutes. Turn down the heat and simmer slowly, adding more water if necessary, until tender (test by pressing a bean between the fingers). Be careful not to overcook the beans.

EGGPLANTS:
Prepare eggplants for cooking by peeling, scooping, chopping or slicing as directed in the recipe, then sprinkle with salt and allow to drain in a colander for at least half an hour or, alternatively, soak in salted water for one hour. Drain and dry with a towel or absorbent paper. These procedures eliminate the eggplants' bitter characteristic and tendency to absorb a great deal of oil during cooking.

HERBS:
Fresh, dried and powdered herbs are used in Lebanese cooking. If you run out of one type it can be substituted by another in the following proportions: 1 tablespoon fresh chopped herbs = 1 teaspoon dried = ½ teaspoon powdered.

Many Lebanese cooks prefer to dry their own herbs, particularly parsley and mint. The method for drying is: Wash and dry the fresh herb. Tie it in a bunch, then hang it upside-down in a draughty place for several weeks until the leaves crumble easily in the hand. Remove the leaves from the stem and crush the leaves to a powder by rubbing them in the palms of the hands. Store in an airtight jar.

HOT PEPPERS:
"Necklaces" of dried red and green hot peppers (chillis) decorate most Lebanese kitchens. They can be used instead of fresh ones in all recipes, provided they are soaked first in hot water until they become

soft. The method for drying is: Wash and dry the hot peppers. Using a large needle and strong thread, sew through the stems to make a "necklace". Hang the necklace in a draughty place until the peppers are completely dried.

HOUMMUS:
Hoummus means chick peas. The dip popularly known as "hoummus" is correctly *Hoummus b'Tahini* (see page 34).

LENTILS:
Before cooking lentils it is advisable to spread them out on a tray and inspect them for pieces of grit, then wash well and drain. They do not need soaking.

MINCER:
A simple mincer (grinder) will be very helpful for preparing many ingredients.

MIXED SPICES:
Spices are generally mixed for use in Lebanese cooking. Where a recipe states **mixed spices** you can use the commercial "Mixed Spice" (which combines allspice, cinnamon, nutmeg and cinnamon oil) or blend your own mixture. Note that "allspice" (pimento) is a reddish brown berry which tastes like a mixture of cinnamon, cloves, nutmeg and juniper and should not be mistaken for Mixed Spice.

Another popular spice mixture in Lebanon is "four spice", a combination of cinnamon, nutmeg, cloves and ginger. A favourite pepper mixture is made up of 2 parts allspice, 2 parts black pepper and 1 part white pepper.

MORTAR AND PESTLE:
A mortar is a vessel in which food is pounded with a pestle. A milk bottle and bread board or rolling pin and bread board are suitable substitutes. Unless otherwise stated, you can use a blender if you prefer.

ORANGE BLOSSOM WATER:
See Rosewater.

PEPPERS:
The red and green peppers (capsicum) used in all recipes must be fresh.

PINE NUTS:
These are the kernels from the cones of the Stone or Umbrella pine *(Pinus pinea)*, a native of the Mediterranean region. They have a distinctive flavour and can be purchased from health food shops and continental delicatessens. Blanched slivered almonds are a suitable substitute in most recipes.

POMEGRANATES:
Pomegranates are a popular and plentiful fruit in the Middle East. The fresh fruit is used for decorating food and a special pomegranate sauce called *Dibbis Rhuman* is often used for flavouring

savoury dishes. This sauce is available at some Lebanese food shops, but as it is not readily procurable elsewhere we have used lemon juice in this book.

RICE:
Any white grain rice may be used. It should be washed and drained before cooking.

ROSEWATER and ORANGE BLOSSOM WATER:
The rosewater and orange blossom water used in this book are the diluted essences available from chemists, drug stores, health food shops and some continental delicatessens. Pure essence, which is much more expensive, may be substituted but the quantities should be reduced to a few drops.

TAHINI:
Tahini is a white, slightly bitter sesame paste made from raw sesame seeds. It can be obtained from continental delicatessens and health food stores and will keep indefinitely. Do not confuse it with the brown, nutty sesame paste made from roasted sesame seeds, which is sold at Chinese stores.

TOMATO PASTE:
Commercial tomato paste can be used for the recipes in this book, however most Lebanese prefer to use the following home-made paste. For a yield of approx 500 g (1 lb): Wash 2.5 kg (5 lb) ripe tomatoes, core out the stem ends and slice into a large pot. Cover and heat gently until soft, then rub through a sieve. Return the juice to the pot and simmer slowly, uncovered, until reduced by half to a tomato purée. Pour into a baking dish, cover with gauze and dry in the sun for 2-4 days, stirring occasionally. (Alternatively, cook in a cool oven for 4-6 hours.) When the tomatoes are the consistency of a soft paste (as commercial tomato paste), stir in 1 tablespoon of salt and spoon into sterilized jars. Pour a layer of oil on top, seal and store in a cool place. When opened, store in the refrigerator.

ZAATAR MIXTURE:
This is a popular herbal blend consisting of 1 part thyme (zaatar), 1 part roasted sesame seeds, ¼ part sim'meh and salt to taste. It can be bought from most Lebanese delicatessens. Thyme is a suitable substitute.

ZUCCHINI SCOOP:
To scoop out zucchini and eggplant for stuffing, a special utensil called *ma'warra* is used (see picture, page 80). This scoop can be purchased from Lebanese importers, or you can make your own using the following method: Cut a 30 cm (12 in) piece of 12 mm (½ in) copper pipe in a lengthwise slope down the middle, so that you have a cut section of 18 cm (7 in) with an uncut section of 12 cm (5 in) which can be used as a handle. Sharpen all the cut edges. An apple corer may be used as a substitute.

EQUIVALENT TERMS

Most culinary terms in the English-speaking world can cross national borders without creating havoc in the kitchen. Nevertheless, local usage can produce some problems. The following list contains names of ingredients, equipment and cookery terms that are used in this book, but which may not be familiar to all readers.

USED IN THIS BOOK	ALSO KNOWN AS
baking powder	double-acting baking powder
baking tray	baking sheet
bicarbonate of soda	baking soda
biscuits	cookies
boiler chicken	stewing chicken
pepper, red or green	sweet or bell pepper, capsicum
caster sugar	fine granulated sugar, superfine sugar
cornflour	cornstarch
desiccated coconut	shredded coconut
essence	extract
eggplant	aubergine
fillet (of meat)	tenderloin
frying pan	skillet
glacé (fruits)	candied
grill/griller	broil/broiler
hard-boiled egg	hard-cooked egg
icing sugar	confectioners' sugar
mincer	grinder
okra	gumbo, ladies' fingers
pastry	pie crust
pinch (of salt)	dash
plain flour	all-purpose flour
rosewater essence	rose extract
self-raising flour	self-rising flour
sieve	strain/strainer
(to) sift	(to) strain
spring onions	scallions, green onions
stone, seed, pip	pit
tea towel	dish towel, glass cloth
(to) whisk	(to) whip, beat
zucchini	courgettes

GUIDE TO WEIGHTS AND MEASURES

The metric weights and metric fluid measures used in this book are those of the **Standards Association of Australia**. A good set of scales, a graduated Australian Standard measuring cup and a set of Australian measuring spoons will be very helpful and can be obtained from leading hardware and kitchenware stores.

All cup and spoon measurements are level:

- The **Australian Standard measuring cup** has a capacity of 250 millilitres (250 ml).
- The **Australian Standard tablespoon** has a capacity of 20 millilitres (20 ml).
- The **Australian Standard teaspoon** has a capacity of 5 millilitres (5 ml).

In all recipes, imperial equivalents of metric measures are shown in parentheses, e.g. 500 g (1 lb) beef. Although the metric yields of cup and weighed measures are approximately 10 per cent greater than the imperial yields, the proportions remain the same. Therefore, for successful cooking use either metric **or** imperial weights and measures — do **not** mix the two.

New Zealand, British, United States and Canadian weights and measures are the same as Australian weights and measures except that:

(a) the Australian and British Standard tablespoons have a capacity of 20 millilitres (20 ml) whereas the New Zealand, United States and Canadian Standard tablespoons have a capacity of 15 millilitres (15 ml), therefore all tablespoon measures should be taken generously in those countries;

(b) the imperial pint (Australia, New Zealand and Britain) has a capacity of 20 fl oz whereas the US pint used in the United States and Canada has a capacity of 16 fl oz, therefore pint measures should be increased accordingly in those two countries.

The following charts of conversion equivalents will be useful:

Imperial Weight	Metric Weight
½ oz	15 g
1 oz	30 g
2 oz	60 g
3 oz	90 g
4 oz (¼ lb)	125 g
6 oz	185 g
8 oz (½ lb)	250 g
12 oz (¾ lb)	375 g
16 oz (1 lb)	500 g
24 oz (1½ lb)	750 g
32 oz (2 lb)	1000 g (1 kg)
3 lb	1500 g (1.5 kg)
4 lb	2000 g (2 kg)

Key: oz = ounce; lb = pound; g = gram; kg = kilogram.

Imperial Liquid Measures	Cup Measures	Metric Liquid Measures
1 fl oz		30 ml
2 fl oz	¼ cup	
3 fl oz		100 ml
4 fl oz (¼ pint US)	½ cup	
5 fl oz (¼ pint imp.)		150 ml
6 fl oz	¾ cup	
8 fl oz (½ pint US)	1 cup	250 ml
10 fl oz (½ pint imp.)	1¼ cups	
12 fl oz	1½ cups	
14 fl oz	1¾ cups	
16 fl oz (1 pint US)	2 cups	500 ml
20 fl oz (1 pint imp.)	2½ cups	

Key: fl oz = fluid ounce; ml = millilitre.

OVEN TEMPERATURE GUIDE

The Celsius and Fahrenheit temperatures in this chart relate to most electric ovens. Decrease by 10°C or 25°F for gas ovens or refer to the manufacturer's temperature guide. For temperatures below 160°C (325°F), do not decrease the given temperature.

Description of oven	Celsius °C	Fahrenheit °F	Gas Mark
Cool	100	200	¼
Very Slow	120	250	½
Slow	150	300	2
Moderately Slow	160	325	3
Moderate	180	350	4
Moderately Hot	190	375	5
Hot	200	400	6
Very Hot	230	450	8

BASIC MIXTURES

Basic mixtures of rice, stuffings, yoghurts, cheese, sauces, pastries and bread form the foundation of all Lebanese cooking. At least one is included in every meal, often as part of another recipe.

The beauty of this style of cooking is that a large amount of food can be made and then stored ready for future meals. This is extremely useful if you intend to eat Lebanese food for a few days or if you are planning a large dinner party and want to get as much work as possible done ahead of time.

Study these recipes well and practise making them, for once they are familiar you will find Lebanese cooking very simple.

Basic ingredients for Lebanese cooking:

1. *Tahini*
2. *Lentils*
3. *Black Pepper*
4. *Pine Nuts*
5. *Cinnamon Sticks*
6. *Bur'ghul*
7. *Chick Peas*
8. *Mixed Spices*
9. *Tomato Paste*
10. *Cream Cheese*
11. *Meat and Rice Stuffing*
12. *Salt*
13. *Lemons, onions, garlic and hot peppers*
14. *Vermicelli*

Note the brass mortar and pestle.

Tahini Sauce
Taratoor b'Tahini Ⓥ Ⓛ

Makes: 2¼ cups
1 clove garlic
½ teaspoon salt
1 cup tahini (see page 21)
approx ½ cup lemon juice
water
½ cup finely chopped parsley (optional)

Crush the garlic and salt together to a paste. Mix in the tahini and beat in the lemon juice. Gradually mix in enough water to make the mixture the consistency of very thick cream or mayonnaise. Add parsley, adjust salt and lemon to taste.

Avocado with Tahini Sauce
Taratoor b'Abocarto Ⓥ Ⓛ

Makes: approx 2 cups
1 large avocado
¾ cup Tahini Sauce (see above)

Peel and mash the avocado and blend in the Tahini Sauce until smooth.

Adjust lemon and salt to taste, if necessary.

Serve with salad vegetables, cold chicken or as a dip for mezza.

Pine Nut Sauce
Taratoor b'Snoobar

This sauce is traditionally served with fish.

Makes: approx ¾ cup
1 slice of soft ordinary bread (not the Lebanese variety) without crust, 1.25 cm (½ in) thick and soaked in 1 cup water
1 clove garlic
½ tablespoon salt
¾ cup pine nuts
approx ½ cup lemon juice
2 tablespoons water

Squeeze the soaked bread to dry.

Crush the garlic and salt together. Pound in the pine nuts to a paste. Pound in the bread, add the lemon juice and water.

Sieve the mixture through a fine strainer.

Adjust salt and lemon to taste.

Alternative method: Place all the ingredients into a blender and blend into a smooth sauce, adding more water if necessary.

Garlic Sauce
Zait b'Toom Ⓥ Ⓛ

Garlic sauce is a delicious accompaniment for grilled chicken or shellfish. It is extremely important that you start crushing the garlic with a mortar and pestle to ensure that the oil will be thoroughly absorbed. Do not add the oil or lemon juice too quickly and always stir in the one direction or the mixture will fall flat.

Makes: approx 2½ cups
all cloves of 1 knob of garlic
1 teaspoon salt
approx 2 cups olive oil
approx ¼ cup lemon juice

Crush the garlic in the salt with a mortar and pestle until the salt is dissolved.

Very gradually add 1 tablespoon of oil (a few drops at a time) and then a few drops of lemon juice and, stirring in the one direction with the pestle, blend into the garlic. When the oil has been completely absorbed into the garlic, very gradually add another tablespoon of oil alternately with a few more drops of lemon juice, continuing in this way until the oil is no longer being absorbed into the garlic.

The mixture should be light and fluffy like whipped cream. If it is not, you can save the day by mixing in a well mashed potato.

Alternative method: After using about 4 tablespoons of olive oil, transfer the mixture to an electric beater and continue the process as above.

Ghee
Sumneh Ⓥ

Ghee is clarified butter. It can be purchased commercially or made at home. Ordinary butter, margarine, nut or vegetable oil may be substituted, but ghee has a distinctive flavour and does not burn easily. Unlike butter or margarine it keeps indefinitely unrefrigerated.

Makes: 1 kg (2 lbs)
Cooking time: approx 20 minutes
1 kg (2 lb) butter

Place butter in a large saucepan, melt and bring to the boil. Allow to boil for a few minutes watching very carefully. As soon as the froth on the surface starts to disperse, remove immediately from heat and allow to cool. Skim off the remainder of froth.

Pour into a glass or earthenware jar, being careful not to pour in the sediment on the bottom.

Variation:
Half margarine can be substituted for half the amount of butter.

Ushta
Thick Clotted Cream Ⓥ

Ushta is the thick layer of clotted cream from the top of rich, boiled goats' milk. Unlike whipped cream it does not melt when cooked or served with hot sweets. A satisfactory substitute can be made with cows' milk and cream, using this recipe.

Makes: 1.25 litres (2½ pints)
Cooking time: approx 1½ hours
1 litre (2 pints) milk
¼ litre (½ pint) cream

Mix the milk and cream together and place in a wide shallow tray on top of the stove. Bring slowly to the boil, then turn down the heat as low as possible and allow the mixture to stand over it for half an hour.

Turn off the heat, cover and leave the mixture to stand for 8 hours before refrigerating. Place in the refrigerator for a further 7 hours.

With a sharp knife, detach the thick layer of cream from around the edges of the pan and lift it off the top of the milk. Place the cream on a platter and slice it into pieces.

Yoghurt
Lubban Ⓥ

In the Lebanese cuisine yoghurt is served in a variety of ways with most meals, but never with fish or tahini. When preparing the yoghurt, temperature conditions must be exactly right and the culture must not be disturbed while it is working.

Makes: 5 cups
Cooking time: approx 20 minutes
1 cup full cream powdered milk
5 cups whole milk (not homogenized)
1 tablespoon plain yoghurt (for starter)

Mix the powdered milk into the fresh milk in a saucepan and heat until it comes to the boil. When boiled, immediately remove from the heat and leave to cool until lukewarm. The mixture should be just warm enough for the yoghurt germ to spread (36°C/97°F). (The traditional way to test this temperature is to immerse the little finger in the milk. You should be able to hold it there for the count of 10, but no longer.)

In a large cup, mix several tablespoons of the warm milk with the starter yoghurt and stir to a smooth paste. Add the paste to the remainder of the warm milk, and stir in gently. Pour the mixture into an enamel or porcelain bowl, cover with a lid or plate, wrap a towel (in summer) or blanket (in winter) around it and allow to stand in a warm place for 6 hours or until set. Remove towel or blanket and refrigerate.

The yoghurt will set like a junket. The taste will vary according to the age of the starter: if the starter is refrigerated for a week or more it will be very tart; if the starter is fresh it will be sweeter.

Variation:
Yoghurt can also be made using instant powdered milk instead of full cream and whole milk. Use 2½ cups of very hot water (not boiling) for every 1½ cups of instant powdered milk. Place them in a bowl and mix well. Test the temperature, mix in the starter, cover and set aside as above.

Cooked Yoghurt

Lubban Mutboukh Ⓥ

When cooking yoghurt it is important to remember that it must not be covered during the cooking process and must always be stirred in the same direction.

Makes: 1.25 litres (2 pints)
Cooking time: 20 minutes

1.25 litres (2 pints) yoghurt
1 egg white, beaten
2 cloves garlic
1 teaspoon salt
1 tablespoon dried mint or coriander
2 heaped teaspoons cornflour/cornstarch (optional)

In a saucepan beat together the yoghurt and beaten egg white. Bring to the boil slowly, stirring constantly in the same direction to avoid burning or curdling.

When the yoghurt comes to the boil add the crushed garlic cloves, salt and dried mint or coriander. If a thicker consistency is required, mix two heaped teaspoons of cornflour/cornstarch to a paste with water and blend into the mixture just before it comes to the boil.

Cream Cheese

Lubbneh Ⓥ

Lubbneh is a favourite Lebanese breakfast when served with olive oil, Zaatar Mixture (see page 21), olives and bread.

Makes: approx ¼ of original quantity of yoghurt

Place a quantity of cold yoghurt in cheese cloth or similar material, tie it into a sack and hang it on the kitchen tap to allow liquid to drain into the sink. Alternatively hang over a bowl.

Remove from cloth after 8 hours. Sprinkle with salt, store in a covered container in refrigerator.

Use as a spread or mould into little balls.

White Cheese

Jibni Byda Ⓥ

Makes: 250 g (½ lb)
Cooking time: 5 minutes

2.5 litres (4 pints) milk (not homogenized)
1 plain junket tablet, dissolved in 1 tablespoon cold water
1 tablespoon salt

Heat the milk until it is just slightly warm. Stir in the dissolved junket tablet and the salt. Leave it to stand uncovered in a warm place until set — approximately 20 minutes.

Break up the curds with a large spoon and pour the mixture into a colander lined with cheese cloth and set in the sink or over a large bowl.

Stir mixture for a few minutes so that the curds separate and the whey drains through the cloth.

When most of the whey has drained off, tie the corners of the cloth into a sack. Return the sack to the colander and set it over a bowl or hang it from a tap over the kitchen sink.

When the whey has completely drained away and the curds become a solid mass (approximately 1-2 hours), turn out into a shallow bowl. Sprinkle with more salt if necessary. Cover and store in refrigerator.

Meat and Nut Filling
Hashweh

Makes: 2 cups
Cooking time: 35 minutes

3 tablespoons ghee or substitute (see page 27)
½ cup pine nuts
2 medium onions, finely chopped
500 g (1 lb) meat, coarsely ground or finely chopped
2 teaspoons salt
¼ teaspoon pepper
½ teaspoon mixed spices (see page 21)
¼ teaspoon ground cinnamon

Heat the ghee in a pan and lightly brown the pine nuts. Remove and set aside.

Add the meat to the ghee and fry for a few minutes until the raw look disappears. Before the meat browns, mix in the chopped onions, salt, pepper, mixed spices and cinnamon. Cover, turn down to medium heat and continue to cook until meat is very tender and the juices are absorbed — approx 20-25 minutes.

Remove from heat and mix in the pine nuts.

Rice Stuffing for Poultry
Hashwit Djaaj b'Ruz

Makes: 4 cups
Cooking time: 25 minutes

3 tablespoons ghee or substitute (see page 27)
¾ cup pine nuts
500 g (1 lb) lean lamb, coarsely ground or finely cubed
1 cup rice, washed and drained
2 teaspoons salt
1 teaspoon pepper
1 teaspoon mixed spices (see page 21)
2 chicken stock cubes (optional)
1¼ cups boiling water

Heat the ghee in a pan and brown the nuts lightly. Remove and set aside.

Add the meat to the ghee and fry for 5 minutes until brown. Stir in the rice, salt, pepper and mixed spices.

Dissolve chicken cubes in boiling water and add to the meat and rice mixture. Simmer uncovered for 5 minutes, then cover tightly and simmer gently for a further 10 minutes.

Mix in the browned nuts.

Meat and Rice Stuffing
Hashwit Mihshi

This stuffing is always used for vegetables.

Makes: 4 cups
Cooking time: 10 minutes

1 medium onion, finely chopped
1 tablespoon ghee or substitute (see page 27)
2 teaspoons salt
1 teaspoon black pepper
1 teaspoon cinnamon or mixed spices (see page 21)
1¼ cups rice, washed and drained
500 g (1 lb) coarsely ground or finely chopped meat (preferably lamb shoulder)
½ cup water

Sauté the onion in the ghee until soft. Mix the onions and ghee, salt, pepper and cinnamon or spices into the rice. Add the meat and water. Mix well.

Lenten Stuffing
Hashu Orteh Ⓥ Ⓛ

This stuffing contains no meat or dairy products and is ideal for vegetarian dishes. It can supplement the filling in all stuffed vegetables, however when used for stuffed tomatoes, omit the chick peas.

Makes: 4 cups

½ cup chick peas, soaked overnight (see page 20)
½ cup chopped mint or 2 teaspoons dried mint
½ cup finely chopped parsley
2 medium tomatoes, chopped
½ cup spring onions, chopped
1¼ cups rice, washed and drained
1 teaspoon salt
¼ teaspoon cinnamon
¼ teaspoon pepper
½ teaspoon Zaatar Mixture (see page 21) or thyme (optional)
1 cup olive or nut oil
3 tablespoons lemon juice

Drain the soaked chick peas and crack them by placing in a clean cloth and rolling with a rolling pin.

Wash and drain the cracked chick peas, place in a bowl and mix in all the remaining ingredients.

Rice Pilaf

Ruz Bish'irreeyeh Ⓥ

Serves: 6-8
Cooking time: 30 minutes

1 cup broken up vermicelli or fine egg noodles
2½ tablespoons ghee or substitute (see page 27)
2 cups rice (preferably long grained), washed
   and drained
1½ teaspoons salt
4 cups boiling water
ground cinnamon

Sauté the vermicelli or noodles in the ghee until a light brown colour, stirring constantly to avoid burning.

Mix the rice and salt well into the vermicelli then add the boiling water. Give one final stir, allow a few seconds to bubble, then cover the rice tightly. Turn heat down to very low and simmer until cooked — approx 20 minutes.

When ready to serve, stir the rice gently with a fork, turn onto serving dish and sprinkle ground cinnamon lightly over the top.

Variations:
• Lightly fried pine nuts may also be sprinkled over the rice.
• When served with chicken, half chicken broth may be substituted for half the amount of water. Alternatively, add 2 chicken stock cubes to the water.

Preparing Bread Cloth. Note the sorj in the foreground of the picture.

Bur'ghul Pilaf

Bur'ghul b'Dfeen Ⓥ

Serves: 4-6
Cooking time: 50 minutes

2 cups bur'ghul, washed and drained (see page 20)
1¼ cups pine nuts to garnish (optional)
½ cup ghee or substitute (see page 27)
1 medium onion, chopped
2 teaspoons salt
¼ teaspoon black pepper
3½ cups meat or chicken broth

Wash the bur'ghul and drain well by squeezing out excess water between cupped hands. Place in a bowl and set aside for half an hour or more.

In a large saucepan, lightly fry the pine nuts in half the ghee, drain and set aside.

Fry the onion in the same ghee until golden brown. Add the remainder of the ghee, heat and stir in the bur'ghul, salt and pepper. Sauté for a few minutes.

In another saucepan, bring the broth to the boil and mix it into the bur'ghul mixture. Allow to bubble for a few seconds. Cover tightly, turn down the heat and simmer very slowly — or place in the oven as a casserole at 180°C (350°F).

The pilaf is cooked when all the stock has been absorbed and the bur'ghul is soft and fluffy — approx 40-50 minutes. (If the stock is absorbed before the bur'ghul is cooked, add a little more *boiling* stock or water and continue cooking.) Allow to stand for at least 15 minutes.

Serve in place of rice and garnish with pine nuts.

Variations:
• Three peeled and chopped tomatoes may be added with the broth but reduce the broth by half a cup.
• Chopped spring onions may be added with the broth.

Lebanese Bread
Khoubiz Ⓥ Ⓛ

Commercially-made Lebanese bread is readily available at delicatessens and food stores. The home-made variety may be lighter in colour and texture because of the temperature limitation of the domestic oven.

Makes: 8 rounds
Cooking time: 4-8 minutes per round

15 g (½ oz) dried yeast or 30 g (1 oz) fresh yeast
2½ cups lukewarm water
1 teaspoon sugar
8 cups plain flour
2 teaspoons salt
3 tablespoons oil

Dissolve the yeast in ¼ cup of the lukewarm water, add sugar and set aside in a warm place until it rises and foams — approx 10-15 minutes.

Sift the flour and salt into a large mixing bowl and place in a warm oven for a few minutes to warm slightly.

Pour the yeast into a well in the centre of the flour and mix it in by hand, adding the water gradually. Knead well to a soft dough.

Turn the dough onto a lightly floured board or cloth and continue to knead until it is smooth and shiny — approx 15-20 minutes.

Knead in 2 tablespoons of the oil, roll into a large ball and rub the remainder of the oil around the ball. Leave in the bowl, cover with a damp cloth and set aside in a warm place to rise until nearly double its size — approx 1-2 hours.

Turn the oven on to maximum heat at least ¾ hour before cooking the bread.

Punch the dough down in the centre and draw edges to the middle to re-form the ball. Turn onto a floured board or cloth and knead for approx 2 minutes.

Divide the dough into 8 equal portions and roll each portion into a ball.

Flatten each ball on a lightly floured cloth and roll with a rolling pin into flat round shapes, about the size of a dinner plate and approx 6 mm (¼ in) thick. Place bread rounds on a lightly floured cloth, cover with another floured cloth and set aside to again rise to nearly double their size — approx 20-30 minutes.

Place a baking tray in the oven for 5 minutes, remove and lightly rub with oil.

Place one round of bread on the baking tray and cook until it swells up in the centre and browns slightly — approx 4-8 minutes. Remove from oven (the swelling will sink immediately) and wrap in a cloth. Continue in this way until all the rounds are cooked.

The bread should be white, soft and chewy. When cut in half it will form a pocket into which sandwich fillings of every description may be placed.

Bread Cloth
Khoubiz Sorj Ⓥ Ⓛ

To make this recipe you will require a sorj. This is a simple convex metal plate measuring between 30 cm (12 in) and 90 cm (36 in) and can be purchased at Lebanese or Indian stores. An ideal substitute is an old plough disc.

Makes: 8-16 rounds, depending on the size of the sorj
Cooking time: 3-5 minutes per round

1 kg (2 lb) Lebanese Bread dough (see left)

After the dough has risen, divide it into about 16 small balls, depending on the size of the sorj.

With a rolling pin, roll each ball out as thinly as possible on a floured cloth. It is not necessary to keep an absolutely round shape but it should be as thin as cloth and have no holes in it.

Place the sorj convexly (dome-like) over a hotplate. When very hot, carefully lift the cloth bread onto it. Leave until cooked through and forming bubbles — approx 3-5 minutes. Peel the bread off the sorj and continue the process until all the bread is cooked.

This bread is used to roll up sandwich fillings of any description.

MEZZA

Mezza is a selection of hors d'oeuvres, often comprising thirty or more small dishes. It is traditionally served as an appetiser, but is sometimes eaten as a meal in itself.

Arack, an anisated alcoholic drink, is always served with the mezza, along with Lebanese bread, which can be torn into small pieces for the dips.

The "home of mezza" is the town of Zahle, situated in the picturesque countryside at the foot of Mount Lebanon. Here the best quality arack is produced and an amazing number of restaurants specialise in mezza.

To make up a mezza you may choose a selection of kibbi, cheese, nuts, raisins, pickles, olives, dips, *Tabbouleh* (see page 88) and other salads, grape vine rolls, various savoury pastries and any of the following recipes.

A selection of mezza dishes.

Hoummus b'Tahini

Chick Pea Dip ⓋⓁ

Makes: approx 3 cups
Cooking time: approx 1½ hours

1½ cups chick peas, soaked overnight (see page 20)
water
2 teaspoons salt
approx 2 cloves garlic
¾ cup tahini (see page 21)
approx ½ cup lemon juice
pinch cayenne pepper and 2 tablespoons chopped
    parsley to garnish

Drain the soaked chick peas, place in a pot and add three times their amount of water. Add 1 teaspoon salt and bring to the boil. Boil vigorously for about 10 minutes, turn the heat down, cover the saucepan and simmer until the chick peas are very soft — approx 1 hour. Drain liquid off and reserve.

Reserve ½ cup of the whole, cooked chick peas for garnish. Purée the remainder of the peas by pressing through a sieve or placing in blender.

Crush the garlic with the remaining teaspoon of salt. Beat or blend it into the purée.

Slowly beat in the tahini and lemon juice alternately. Blend in a little of the reserved liquid to make the mixture a thick creamy consistency. Adjust salt and lemon to taste.

Serve on a platter garnished with a pinch of cayenne pepper, parsley and the reserved chick peas.

Baba Ghannouj

Eggplant and Tahini Dip ⓋⓁ

Makes: 1 mezza dish
Cooking time: 20 minutes

1 large eggplant
approx ¼ cup lemon juice
4-5 tablespoons tahini (see page 21)
2 cloves garlic
1½ teaspoons salt
¼ cup finely chopped parsley to garnish

Remove the green from around the neck of the eggplant, but leave the stem. Place in a hot oven until soft — approx 15-20 minutes — or hold onto stem and place over open grill or hotplate, turning from time to time until eggplant has softened. Allow to cool.

Remove the skin carefully, while holding the stem. Mash the pulp thoroughly with a fork or place in the blender and slowly beat in lemon juice alternately with tahini.

Crush garlic with salt and mix to a paste. Blend into the eggplant mixture. Adjust salt.

Pour into shallow serving dishes or platters and garnish with chopped parsley. Serve with Lebanese bread.

Fried Eggplant

Batinjaan Mi'li ⓋⓁ

Makes: 1 mezza dish
Cooking time: 10-15 minutes

1 medium eggplant
olive or nut oil for frying
salt and pepper
juice of 1 lemon

Peel the eggplant, slice into 5 mm (¼ in) circles and prepare for cooking (see page 20).

Fry sliced eggplant in oil until browned on both sides and soft inside. Drain on absorbent paper.

Sprinkle with salt, pepper and lemon juice, and serve warm or cold with bread.

Fried Cauliflower

Ar'nabit Mi'li ⓋⓁ

Makes: 1 mezza dish
Cooking time: approx 20 minutes

1 small cauliflower
olive or nut oil for frying
salt and pepper
juice of 1 lemon

Separate the cauliflower in flowerettes and deep fry in oil until golden brown and tender. Drain on absorbent paper.

Sprinkle with salt, pepper and lemon juice. Serve warm or cold.

Fried Chicken Giblets in Lemon Juice

Bearsheart Mi'leeyeh

Makes: 1 mezza dish
Cooking time: 25 minutes

2 cups chicken giblets
2 tablespoons ghee or substitute (see page 27)
2 medium onions, chopped finely
2 cloves garlic, crushed
salt
pepper
½ teaspoon mixed spices (see page 21)
juice of 1 lemon
¼ cup finely chopped parsley

Wash the giblets, then sauté in hot ghee until brown and nearly cooked through — approx 15 minutes. Add the chopped onions and garlic and continue to sauté until the onions are soft. Mix in the salt, pepper and mixed spices, then the lemon juice and sauté for a few more minutes.

Serve warm or cold, garnished with parsley.

Fried Kidneys in Lemon Juice

Kar'laerwe Mi'leeyeh

Makes: 1 mezza dish
Cooking time: ½ hour

12 lamb kidneys or 5 beef kidneys
salt and pepper
½ cup ghee or substitute (see page 27)
2 tablespoons plain flour
¾ cup lemon juice
1 teaspoon dried mint

Wash and dry kidneys. Split lengthwise and remove skin. Flatten with a pestle or rolling pin and sprinkle with salt and pepper.

Melt ghee in a pan and fry kidneys until brown on both sides. Remove kidneys.

Add flour to pan, lower heat and stir until it begins to turn brown. Add lemon juice and bring to the boil.

Return kidneys to pan, add dried mint and allow to simmer in the sauce for a few minutes.

Marinated Lambs' Brains

N'kha m'Tabbal

Makes: 1 mezza dish
Cooking time: 10-15 minutes

6 sets lambs' brains
salt
water
1 teaspoon vinegar
lemon wedge
¼ cup olive oil
½ cup lemon juice
½ cup chopped spring onions
pepper
¼ cup finely chopped parsley to garnish

If brains are fresh, remove skin (this is easier if soaked for half an hour in cold water, a little salt and a tablespoon of vinegar). If brains are frozen, leave unskinned as the skin will be too difficult to remove.

Simmer brains gently in salted water with a teaspoon of vinegar and a lemon wedge until tender — approx 10-15 minutes. Drain well and cool.

Cut brains into narrow strips and place in a small serving dish. Make a mixture with the olive oil, lemon juice, spring onions and pepper. Adjust salt. Pour over the brains, garnish with chopped parsley, and refrigerate.

Serve chilled.

Fried Lamb's Liver

Kibid Mi'li

Makes: 1 mezza dish
Cooking time: 15-20 minutes

1 lamb's fry/liver
½ cup olive or nut oil
salt and pepper
juice of 1 lemon
1 tablespoon chopped parsley to garnish

Cut the lamb's fry into 2.5 cm (1 in) strips, discarding the gristle. Fry in hot oil to brown the outside and lightly cook inside.

Chop into cubes and serve warm or cold, sprinkled with lemon juice and garnished with parsley.

Marinated Tongue Salad

L'sanaat m'Tabli

Makes: 1 mezza dish
Cooking time: 2½ hours

4 sheep's tongues or 1 small beef tongue
1 large carrot, chopped finely
1 large onion, chopped finely
2 spring onions, chopped finely
1 teaspoon salt
1 cup water
½ cup lemon juice
¼ cup olive oil
1 clove garlic crushed in ½ teaspoon salt
½ cup finely chopped parsley to garnish

Place the tongues in a saucepan, cover with cold water and bring to the boil. Turn down the heat and simmer for 1½ hours.

Drain off water, skin tongues and chop into pieces. Place in saucepan with carrots, onion, spring onions, salt and water. Bring to the boil, turn down the heat and simmer until tender.

Drain saucepan and pour tongues and vegetables into a serving bowl.

Make a dressing with lemon juice, oil and garlic crushed in salt. Pour over the drained tongues and vegetables, garnish with parsley and refrigerate.

Serve cold.

SAVOURY PASTRIES

Savoury pastries are a popular feature of Lebanese cuisine. They come in a variety of shapes and sizes, and the fillings are almost limitless.

We have selected the traditional pastry recipes. They are surprisingly easy to make and can be varied in size, shape and filling as desired.

Savoury pastries are excellent for mezza or light snacks, but may also be served as part of the main course. They are best when piping hot, but are still delicious warm. Whichever way you serve them, make sure they are plentiful because they always disappear quickly!

A platter of delicious Lebanese savoury pastries. From front to back are Lahem b'Ajeen (page 38), Spinach Turnovers (page 39) and Mahnoosh b'Zaatar (page 39).

Simple Pastry ⓥ

This is the traditional Lebanese savoury pastry. However, any commercial or home-made bread dough or filo pastry may be substituted.

Makes: 500 g (1 lb)
2½ cups self-raising flour
½ teaspoon salt
2 tablespoons ghee or substitute (see page 27)
approx ¾ cup water

Sift the flour and salt together and rub in the ghee. Add the water gradually to make a soft dough.

Knead until smooth, adding more water if necessary.

Cover with a damp cloth and place in refrigerator for half an hour before rolling out.

Lahem b'Ajeen

Meat Pastry Rolls

Makes: 30
Cooking time: 15 minutes
2 cups Meat and Nut Filling (see page 29)
approx 2 tablespoons vinegar
approx 2 tablespoons lemon juice
500 g (1 lb) Simple Pastry (see above)
¼ cup ghee or substitute (see page 27)

Place the Meat and Nut Filling in a bowl and mix in the vinegar and lemon juice.

Take one small ball of pastry at a time and roll into a thin sheet on a floured board. Cut into strips approx 7.5cm x 10cm (3in x 4in).

Place 2 teaspoons of filling along the centre of each pastry strip. Roll up firmly and place on a well greased baking tray.

Brush the top of each roll with melted ghee and bake in a moderately hot oven until golden.

Assembling Lahem b'Ajeen pastries.

Variations:
• Instead of a roll, make a tart shape by cutting out small thin rounds of pastry with a biscuit cutter and pulling up and pinching the edges all around to form a round shell.
• Add 2 tablespoons of tomato paste, ½ cup of well strained, peeled, chopped tomatoes and 2 tablespoons of parsley to the Meat and Nut Filling (extra salt may also be necessary).
• Substitute a mixture of 1½ cups minced, steamed brains or cooked chicken, 1 tablespoon finely chopped parsley or spring onions, 1 unbeaten egg, salt and pepper for the Meat and Nut Filling.
• Substitute a mixture of 1½ cups grated cheese, 1 tablespoon parsley and a pinch of cayenne pepper for the Meat and Nut Filling.

Spinach Turnovers

Fa'toy'yeh b'Sbaanegh Ⓥ Ⓛ

This recipe requires only the leaves of the spinach. Use the stalks for the salad recipe on page 89.

Makes: 24 turnovers
Cooking time: 20 minutes

1 kg (2 lb) Lebanese Bread dough (see page 31) or any commercial bread dough
olive or nut oil for baking
Filling:
2 cups finely chopped spinach leaves
½ cup finely chopped parsley
¼ cup finely chopped fresh mint or 1 teaspoon dried mint
½ cup finely chopped spring onions
¼ cup pine nuts, lightly fried in olive oil (optional)
1½ teaspoons salt
¼ teaspoon pepper
¼ teaspoon mixed spices (see page 21)
½ teaspoon Zaatar Mixture (see page 21) or thyme
¼ cup olive oil
approx ¼ cup lemon juice

Place the bread dough in a warm place and allow to rise.

Mix all the filling ingredients together.

When the bread dough has risen, roll out on a floured board to 6 mm (¼ in) thickness and cut in 10 cm (4 in) squares.

Place a tablespoon of filling on each square of dough and fold to form a triangle-shaped pie. Secure edges together by folding them over and pressing firmly down with fork prongs.

Place the pies on a well oiled baking tray and brush each one with oil. Bake in a hot oven, 220°C (425°F) until lightly golden.

Serve hot or cold.

Fried Meat and Pine Nut Pies

Sambousik

Makes: 30 small pies
Cooking time: 3-4 minutes each

2 cups Meat and Nut Filling (see page 29)
approx 2 tablespoons lemon juice
approx 2 tablespoons vinegar
500 g (1 lb) Simple Pastry (see left)
olive oil or substitute

Place the Meat and Nut Filling in a bowl and mix in the lemon juice and vinegar.

Roll out the pastry to about 3 mm (⅛ in) thickness. Cut into small rounds about 7.5 cm (3 in) in diameter.

Place 1½ teaspoons of filling on each pastry round and fold the pastry over it to form a semi-circle shaped pie. Pinch the edges firmly together.

Deep fry in oil until golden.

Serve piping hot.

Mahnoosh b'Zaatar

Herb Rounds Ⓥ Ⓛ

Makes: 8 rounds
Cooking time: 10-15 minutes per batch

1 kg (2 lb) Lebanese Bread dough (see page 31)
¾ cup olive or nut oil
¾ cup Zaatar Mixture (see page 21)

When the bread dough has risen, punch it down and knead again for 2 minutes. Divide it into 8 equal portions and roll each portion into a ball.

Flatten the dough balls on a floured cloth and with a rolling pin roll into little rounds about the size of a small bread and butter plate and 1.25 cm (½ in) thick. Place bread rounds on a lightly floured cloth, cover with another floured cloth and set aside to rise to nearly double their size — 20-30 minutes. Make indents in the rounds by prodding with the finger. Pour oil over the surface and sprinkle liberally with Zaatar Mixture.

Bake in a very hot oven, 240°C (500°F) until cooked — approx 10-15 minutes.

These rounds should be very soft in texture so they can be eaten either rolled up (see picture, page 36) or torn into pieces.

SOUPS

Lebanese soups are very substantial. Rich with meat, grain, legumes and other vegetables, they are considered a meal in themselves but are sometimes served with a variety of dishes as part of the main course.

Like most parts of this cuisine, Lebanese soups keep well and the flavour is not spoiled by reheating. This is particularly useful in the cold winter months because a big cauldron of nourishing soup can always be on hand.

The following soups are the most popular in Lebanon and include several lenten recipes which use neither meat nor dairy products. Bread is always served with them.

A hearty helping of Bur'ghul and Lentil Soup (page 45).

Basic Meat Broth

Makes: 2.5 litres (4 pints)
Cooking time: 1½-2 hours

1.25 kg (2½ lb) soup meat, cubed
several soup bones, cracked
¼ cup ghee or substitute (see page 27)
2.5 litres (4 pints) water
1 tablespoon salt

In a large saucepan lightly brown the meat and bones in the ghee, drain. Pour in the water, add the salt and bring to the boil. Skim fat off the top.

Cover saucepan, turn down heat and simmer, adding more water if necessary. Cook until meat is tender enough to fall off the bones — approx 1½-2 hours.

Spinach Soup

Shourbet Sbaanegh

Serves: 8
Cooking time: 1 hour plus 1½ hours for Basic Meat Broth

2.5 litres (4 pints) Basic Meat Broth plus meat (see above)
750 g (1½ lb) Basic Kibbi Mixture (see page 56)
½ cup ghee or substitute (see page 27)
1 medium onion, chopped finely
1 stick celery, chopped finely
6 cloves garlic, crushed with salt
½ cup rice, washed and drained
1 kg (2 lb) spinach, chopped finely
salt

Remove meat from broth and set aside.

Mould the kibbi into small balls and flatten into patties 2.5 cm (1 in) in diameter. Fry them in half the ghee, drain and set aside.

Brown the chopped onion in the remainder of the ghee, add the celery and garlic. Simmer this mixture for 2 minutes and stir it into the broth.

Bring the broth to the boil, add the rice and continue to simmer for 10 minutes. Bring back to the boil, add the kibbi patties, the spinach and the meat, and simmer for a further 10 minutes or until rice is cooked. Add salt to taste.

White Bean Soup

Shourbet Fassoolia Byda

Serves: 8
Cooking time: 1 hour plus 1½ hours for Basic Meat Broth

1 kg (2 lb) white beans, soaked overnight (see page 20)
4 spring onions
¼ cup ghee or substitute (see page 27)
2.5 litres (4 pints) Basic Meat Broth plus meat (see left)
1 teaspoon salt

Boil the soaked beans for 30 minutes and drain.

Fry the spring onions in the ghee and add to the broth along with the cooked, drained beans and salt.

Bring the soup to the boil, cover and simmer until all the ingredients are soft — approx 30 minutes. Sieve or blend into a purée. Adjust salt to taste.

Reheat before serving.

Meatball Soup

Shourbet El Eema

Serves: 8
Cooking time: ¾ hour plus 1½ hours for Basic Meat Broth

2½ cups ground meat
1¼ teaspoons salt
¼ teaspoon pepper
¼ teaspoon mixed spices (see page 21)
¼ cup ghee or substitute (see page 27)
2.5 litres (4 pints) Basic Meat Broth plus meat (see left)
½ cup tomato juice or 1 tablespoon tomato paste mixed with ½ cup water
½ cup rice
¼ cup chopped parsley
¼ teaspoon cinnamon

Mix the ground meat with the salt, pepper and mixed spices. Shape into balls the size of marbles and brown in hot ghee.

Bring the Basic Meat Broth to the boil, add the meatballs, tomato juice and rice and simmer until the meatballs are cooked through — approximately 20–30 minutes.

Add parsley and cinnamon just before serving. Adjust seasonings to taste.

Chicken and Rice Soup
Shourbet Djaaj b'Ruz

This is one of the lighter Lebanese soups and has a distinctly lemony-garlic flavour.

Serves: 6-8
Cooking time: 1¾ hours

1 large chicken, including giblets
3-4 celery stalks, chopped
2 leeks, sliced (optional)
2-3 cloves garlic, slivered
9 cups water
salt and black pepper
1 cinnamon stick
juice of 1-2 lemons
¾ cup rice, washed and drained
½ cup finely chopped parsley to garnish

Place chicken, giblets, celery, leeks, garlic and water in a pot and bring to the boil. Skim off the top.

Add salt, pepper, cinnamon and the juice of 1 lemon to the soup broth. Cover and simmer until chicken is very tender.

Remove bones, leaving only chicken pieces in the broth. Return to heat, bring to the boil, add the rice and simmer until rice is cooked.

Adjust seasoning, adding more lemon if necessary. Garnish with chopped parsley.

Variation:
When soup is cooked, remove from heat. In a bowl, beat 3 eggs well with the juice of a lemon. Add a ladleful of the soup to the egg and lemon mixture, beat it in well. Pour this back into the pot of soup slowly, beating constantly. Return to *very low* heat and cook gently, stirring constantly until it thickens. *Do not allow the soup to boil* or the eggs will curdle. Adjust seasonings, adding more lemon juice if necessary. Garnish with chopped parsley and serve immediately.

Stuffed Chicken and Soup
Shourbet Djaaj Mihshi

Serves: 4-6
Cooking time: 1½-2 hours

1 boiler chicken
2 cups Rice Stuffing for Poultry (see page 29)
1 cup ghee or substitute (see page 27)
3 teaspoons salt
½ teaspoon black pepper
1 cinnamon stick
¼ cup rice, washed and drained

Lightly stuff the chicken (including the skin of the neck cavity), allowing for rice expansion — approx 1½ cups stuffing. Sew up the openings with coarse white cotton thread.

Brown the chicken all over in ghee.

Place the browned chicken in a large pot, cover with water and add salt, pepper and cinnamon stick. Bring to the boil.

Skim the top of the broth, turn the heat down, cover the saucepan and simmer until nearly cooked — approx 1 hour. Add the rice and remainder of the stuffing to the broth and continue cooking until the chicken is very tender — approx ½ hour.

Remove the chicken and cinnamon stick from the broth. Remove the cotton, cut the chicken into pieces and keep warm.

Skim the fat from the top of the broth and adjust the salt to taste.

Serve the broth in individual bowls, and place the chicken and stuffing on a platter in the centre of the table.

Cold Yoghurt Soup
Kh'yaar b'Lubban Ⓥ

Serves: 4

2 small cucumbers, peeled and sliced
salt
2 cups yoghurt
1-2 cloves garlic, crushed with a pinch of salt
3 tablespoons finely chopped fresh mint or
    2 teaspoons dried mint

Sprinkle the sliced cucumber with salt and set aside in a colander to drain.

Beat the yoghurt with an egg beater until smooth. Beat in the crushed garlic and stir in the mint and drained cucumber. Adjust salt to taste.

Serve chilled.

Pumpkin Soup
Shourbet ya'Teen

Serves: 8
Cooking time: ¾ hour plus 1½ hours for Basic
Meat Broth

2.5 litres (4 pints) Basic Meat Broth plus meat (see page 42)
1.25 kg (2½ lb) pumpkin, peeled and sliced
1 tablespoon ghee or substitute (see page 27)
2 tablespoons plain flour

Bring the Basic Meat Broth to the boil. Add the pumpkin and cook slowly until tender — approx 30 minutes. Remove from heat.

Melt ghee in a small saucepan and add the flour, stirring gently until the flour begins to brown. Add a little broth to the flour mixture and stir well.

Transfer the flour mixture to the broth and pumpkin. Purée with a strainer or blender, return to the heat and bring back to the boil. Adjust seasonings.

Serve immediately.

Lentil and Spinach Soup
Adas b'Sbaanegh Ⓥ Ⓛ

This recipe requires eight spinach leaves but only a few stalks. Use the remaining stalks for the salad recipe on page 89.

Serves: 4-6
Cooking time: 1 hour

1½ cups brown or green lentils, prepared and washed (see page 21)
7 cups water
2 cloves garlic crushed with 1½ teaspoons salt
¾ cup onions, chopped
½ cup olive oil
8 spinach leaves plus a few stalks, chopped finely
½ cup lemon juice
1 teaspoon cornflour/cornstarch (optional)
1 stalk of celery, chopped finely

Place the lentils in a saucepan with 7 cups of water, bring to the boil. Cover and simmer until tender.

Brown the onions in oil. Add the chopped spinach and the garlic crushed with salt, and mix well. Sauté slowly until the spinach becomes soft.

Bring the lentils back to the boil and add the celery and the sautéed mixture. Turn the heat to low and simmer slowly for 5 minutes.

For a thin soup, mix in the lemon juice and adjust salt to taste. For a thicker soup, mix the cornflour/cornstarch with the lemon juice before adding it to the cooked soup, then allow soup to simmer for a few minutes longer.

Wheat Ball and Lentil Soup
Kibbit'healeh Ⓥ Ⓛ

Serves: 8
Cooking time: 1 hour

2 cups bur'ghul, washed and drained (see page 20)
1 cup plain flour
1 tablespoon salt
¼ teaspoon chilli powder
1 cup spring onions, finely chopped
¼ cup mint, finely chopped
½ cup parsley, finely chopped
9 cups water
1 cup brown or green lentils, prepared and washed (see page 21)
4 large spinach leaves, chopped finely
1 large potato, cut in small cubes
½ cup lemon juice
2-4 cloves garlic, crushed
½ cup olive oil

Mix together the bur'ghul, flour, ½ tablespoon salt, chilli powder, spring onions, mint and parsley. Add enough water to make a thick dough. Mould the dough into small balls (about the size of large marbles) and set aside.

Place the lentils in the water, bring to the boil and continue boiling for 10 minutes. Add the chopped spinach, potato and remainder of the salt. Turn heat down and simmer until lentils are tender — approx 20-25 minutes. (At this stage the soup should be the consistency of medium thick soup. If it is too thick, thin it with boiling water).

Bring the soup to the boil and while bubbling add the wheat balls and half the lemon juice. Continue to boil for 5 minutes, add the remainder of the lemon juice, the crushed garlic and the olive oil. Turn down the heat and simmer until the wheat balls are cooked through — approx 10 minutes. Adjust salt and lemon to taste.

Serve hot or cold.

Bur'ghul and Lentil Soup

M'judra Humra Ⓥ Ⓛ

Serves: 6-8
Cooking time: 2 hours

2 cups brown or green lentils, prepared and washed (see page 21)
10 cups water
3 medium onions, cut into fine rings
¾ cup olive oil
2 cups bur'ghul, washed and drained (see page 20)
2 tablespoons salt

Boil the lentils in the water until soft.

Fry the onions in the oil until very dark brown (practically black).

Add the bur'ghul to the cooked lentils and bring to the boil. While boiling slowly add the hot oil from the onions. Add salt. Cover and simmer slowly.

Set the drained, browned onion rings aside and when dry and crisp, crush into a paste.

Mix the onion paste into the simmering lentil and bur'ghul mixture. Continue to simmer until bur'ghul is soft — approx 1½-2 hours. The soup must be *stirred regularly while cooking* to prevent it sticking to the bottom, and boiling water may be added if required to keep a thick, creamy consistency.

Adjust salt to taste.

Variation:
Purée the soup and add lemon juice to taste.

Bean and Grain Soup

Makh'loota Ⓥ Ⓛ

Serves: 4-6
Cooking time: 1¼ hours

½ cup chick peas, soaked overnight (see page 20)
½ cup red or black beans, soaked overnight (see page 20)
½ cup brown or green lentils, prepared and washed (see page 21)
9 cups water
1 tablespoon salt
½ cup bur'ghul, washed and drained (see page 20)
¼ cup rice, washed and drained
1 large onion, sliced finely
½ cup olive or nut oil

Drain the soaked chick peas and beans and place in a large saucepan with the lentils, water and salt. Bring to the boil, cover and simmer vigorously for 30 minutes. Add the bur'ghul and rice.

Fry the finely sliced onions in the oil until they are reddish-brown, then pour both the onions and the very hot oil into the simmering bean and grain mixture.

Cover the mixture and continue to simmer, stirring occasionally, until the rice and bur'ghul are cooked — approx 35-40 minutes. Turn down the heat to very low and cook for a further 10 minutes, adding more water if necessary.

Adjust salt to taste.

FISH

The waters off the coast of Lebanon offer a wealth of seafood, so it is not surprising that fish forms the basis of many popular recipes. It is generally cooked whole and served with a special spicy rice (see page 49) or fried potatoes and Tahini Sauce or Pine Nut Sauce (see page 26).

To prepare for cooking, clean and scale the fish, leaving on the head but removing the eyes. Salt inside and out, then refrigerate for several hours. Allow it to return to room temperature before cooking.

Lebanese fish dishes are always garnished with wedges of lemon and small pieces of Lebanese bread fried in the same oil as the fish. Accompaniments include small pieces of fried vegetables such as cauliflower, zucchini and eggplant, and dips such as *Hoummus b'Tahini* and *Baba Ghannouj* (see page 34).

Baked Fish (page 48), Baked Fish in Tahini Sauce (page 49) and a platter of Sumak Mi'li with fried potatoes, eggplant and cauliflower (page 48).

Sumak Mi'li
Fried Fish

Serves: 4
Cooking time: 10-15 minutes
4 small whole fish or 1 large fish cut into pieces
flour
olive or nut oil

Prepare fish as directed on page 47.

Dredge fish in flour and deep or shallow fry in oil until golden brown and cooked through. Remove and leave to drain off excess oil.

Serve accompanied by Tahini Sauce or Pine Nut Sauce (see page 26), small pieces of fried cauliflower, and Lebanese bread fried in the oil in which the fish was cooked.

Seeyadeeyeh
Fish and Rice Stew

Serves: 4-6
Cooking time: 1½ hours
1 fish, approx 2 kg (4 lb)
½ cup pine nuts
1¼ cups olive or nut oil
2 medium onions, cut into rings
7½ cups water
2½ teaspoons salt
2½ cups rice
½ teaspoon cumin
¼ cup lemon juice
parsley sprigs to garnish

Prepare the fish as directed on page 47.

Lightly brown the pine nuts in ¼ cup of the oil, remove, drain and set aside. Add the remaining oil and fry the onions until very dark brown (but not burnt). Remove the onions and allow to drain.

Place the water in a large saucepan and bring to the boil. Add the onions and continue boiling until soft. Remove the onions from the saucepan and purée through a sieve or strainer back into the boiling water.

Place the fish in the boiling water and add the salt. Simmer until cooked — approx 40 minutes.

Remove the fish from the broth, fillet and keep warm.

Place 5 cups of the broth and the oil in which the onions were fried in another saucepan, bring to the boil and add the rice and cumin. Cover and simmer slowly until rice is cooked and fluid is absorbed — approx 20 minutes.

Make a sauce with 2 cups of the broth and the lemon juice.

Place the fish on a large platter with the rice. Garnish with parsley and pine nuts and serve accompanied by the sauce.

Fish Stew
Yakh'nit Sumak

Serves: 5
Cooking time: 30 minutes
1 fish, approx 1 kg (2 lb)
2 cups olive oil
2 medium onions, sliced
salt
¼ teaspoon saffron
½ cup lemon juice

Prepare the fish as directed on page 47.

Brown fish lightly in olive oil — do *not* cook through. Remove fish and place in saucepan.

Brown the onions in the same oil and drain well.

Mix the onions, salt, saffron and lemon juice, and add to the fish with enough water to cover. Simmer gently until the fish is very tender.

When the fish is cooked, lift it out and remove the flesh from the bones. Lay the fish fillets on a platter.

Season the sauce and pour over the fish. Serve with Spicy Rice for Fish (see right).

Baked Fish
Sumki Makh'boozeh

Serves: 4-6
Cooking time: 40 minutes
1 large whole fish, approx 2.5 kg (5 lb)
¼ cup olive or nut oil
2 lemons cut into round slices
chopped parsley to garnish

Prepare fish as directed on page 47.

Rub fish well with olive or nut oil. Place on a layer of lemon rings in a baking dish. Cook in a moderate oven for 30 minutes, turn over and continue cooking for a further 10 minutes or until flesh is white.

Serve garnished with chopped parsley and accompanied by Tahini Sauce or Pine Nut Sauce (see page 26).

Baked Peppered Fish

Sumki Har'rah

Serves: 4
Cooking time: 45 minutes

1 whole fish, approx 2-2.5 kg (4-5 lb)
¾ cup olive or nut oil
2 medium onions, finely chopped
1 large green pepper, finely chopped
½ hot pepper, finely chopped (optional)
½ teaspoon freshly ground black pepper
¾ cup walnut pieces, finely crushed
1 cup finely chopped parsley
2 cups Tahini Sauce (see page 26)
1 lemon cut into thick slices for garnish

Prepare the fish as directed on page 27.

Pour ¼ cup of the oil into a shallow baking dish. Place the fish in the dish, pour another ¼ cup of oil over it and leave at room temperature for 15 minutes.

Gently heat the remaining oil in a large, heavy frying pan. Add the onions and cook for about 10 minutes, stirring frequently, until they are soft and golden brown. Stir in the green pepper, hot green pepper, black pepper and walnuts and cook for 2-3 minutes until the peppers are soft. Turn off the heat and add ½ cup parsley.

Without removing the fish from the baking dish, fill it with the walnut mixture. Close the opening with small skewers and criss-cross kitchen string around them to secure.

Bake the fish in the centre of a moderate oven, 180°C (350°F), basting it every 15 minutes until cooked (when it feels firm to touch or flakes easily when prodded with a fork) — approx 40-50 minutes.

Remove skewers and spread fish evenly with Tahini Sauce. Sprinkle with the remainder of the parsley and garnish with lemon slices.

Serve hot or cold.

Variation:

For Baked Walnut Fish *(Sumki b'Jose)* omit 1 of the onions, the hot pepper and the Tahini Sauce. You may also like to reduce the amount of black pepper and increase the walnuts.

Baked Fish in Tahini Sauce

Sumki b'Tahini

Serves: 2
Cooking time: approx 40 minutes

1 whole fish, approx 1 kg (2 lb)
½ cup olive or nut oil
1 medium onion, chopped
1 cup Tahini Sauce without parsley (see page 26)
¼ cup finely chopped parsley and wedges of
   lemon to garnish

Prepare fish as directed on page 47.

Rub the fish with half the olive oil and bake in a moderate oven until cooked. The flesh should be white and flake apart easily under a fork.

Fry onions lightly in the remainder of the oil, until transparent. Drain. Mix the onions into the Tahini Sauce, pour over the baked fish and bake for a further 10 minutes in a moderate oven.

Garnish with chopped parsley and wedges of lemon. Serve hot with Spicy Rice for Fish (see below) or cold with salads.

Spicy Rice for Fish

Ruz Lissumak

For added fish flavour, oil left over from frying fish may be used in this recipe.

Serves: 4-6
Cooking time: 30 minutes

½ cup olive or nut oil
¼ cup pine nuts
1 cup onions, sliced
2 cups rice, washed and drained
1 teaspoon salt
3½ cups boiling water
¼ teaspoon powdered saffron

Heat the oil in a saucepan and lightly fry the pine nuts. Remove and set aside.

Lightly brown the onions in the same oil. Add the rice and salt, and sauté for a few minutes.

Pour in the boiling water and saffron. Allow to bubble for a few seconds, cover tightly and turn down to a low simmer. Cook until all the water is absorbed and the rice is tender — approx 20 minutes.

To serve, turn onto a platter, sprinkle with the pine nuts and garnish with fish pieces. Alternatively, serve as an accompaniment to a fish dish.

POULTRY

Originally the Lebanese raised chickens for eggs rather than meat, and only older birds were butchered. To improve the flavour of the "tough old hen" and keep it moist they developed recipes with tasty stuffings, spices and herbs — ideal for enhancing the taste of modern mass-produced chickens.

Roasted pigeons and larks are a great delicacy in Lebanon, however as these birds are protected in Western countries the recipes have been withheld.

Poultry for Lebanese dishes is always prepared by washing and drying well, then rubbing with salt inside and out. Unless otherwise stated it is cooked whole, but it is always served in pieces on a large platter.

Chicken with Chick Peas and Rice (page 52) and Stuffed Roast Chicken (page 53).

Barbecued Garlic Chicken

Djaaj Mishwi

Serves: 2
Cooking time: approx 20 minutes
1 small tender chicken
4 cloves garlic, crushed
1 teaspoon salt
juice of ½ lemon
½ cup of olive oil

Cut the chicken in half or quarters.

Mix the remaining ingredients together to make a marinade sauce. Reserve ¼ cup of this sauce and rub the remainder into the chicken. Leave to marinate for 2-4 hours.

Barbecue or grill the chicken, basting it frequently with the reserved marinade.

Serve hot, accompanied by Garlic Sauce (see page 26) and salads.

Chicken on Skewers

Djaaj Mishwi b'See'arh

Serves: 2-4
Cooking time: 10-15 minutes
2 small chickens
1 cup onions, finely grated
6 cloves garlic, crushed
1 cup lemon juice
3 tablespoons olive oil
salt

Bone the chicken and cut the meat into cubes suitable for skewering.

Blend the onion and garlic into the lemon juice and olive oil. Add salt and marinate the chicken pieces in this mixture for 2-4 hours, turning occasionally.

Remove the chicken from the marinade and thread closely together on skewers. Barbecue for 10-15 minutes, preferably over charcoal.

Serve with Garlic Sauce (see page 26), Hoummus b'Tahini or Baba Ghannouj (see page 34), and Tabbouleh (see page 88).

Chicken with Chick Peas and Rice

D'jaaj b'Hoummus ou Ruz

The ideal pasta for this recipe is the very small Risone No. 63, which resembles brown rice. It is available at continental delicatessens and some supermarkets. Broken up vermicelli is a suitable substitute.

Serves: 4-6
Cooking time: 1½ hours
1 large chicken
1 cup ghee or substitute (see page 27)
12 cups water
2 medium onions, finely chopped
1 clove garlic, crushed
1 cinnamon stick
4 teaspoons salt
¾ cup chick peas, soaked overnight (see page 20)
500 g (1 lb) coarsely ground meat
½ teaspoon cinnamon
½ teaspoon black pepper
¾ cup Risone Pasta No. 63 or broken up vermicelli
1 cup rice, washed and drained
½ cup slivered almonds

In a large saucepan, brown the chicken in ¼ cup of the ghee. Add 8 cups of water, half the chopped onions, the garlic, cinnamon stick and 2 teaspoons salt. Bring to the boil, cover and continue to cook until chicken is tender enough for the meat to fall off the bones.

While the chicken is cooking, drain the soaked chick peas and place in a large pot with 4 cups water. Bring to the boil, cover and simmer vigorously until just tender. Drain and set aside.

In another saucepan, lightly brown the almonds in a little ghee. Remove and set aside.

Add ¼ cup of the ghee to the saucepan and heat. Fry the meat in the ghee, stirring occasionally, until brown all over. Turn down heat to simmer and cook until nearly tender — approx 15 minutes.

Stir in the cinnamon, black pepper and the remainder of the onions and salt, and continue to cook for a further 25 minutes. Remove from saucepan and set aside.

Place the remaining ½ cup of ghee in the same saucepan and sauté the pasta or vermicelli until golden brown. Add the rice and sauté for a few more minutes.

Pour 5 cups of the boiling broth from the cooked chicken over the rice (make up quantity with water if necessary). Bring to the boil and add the cooked meat and onion mixture and the cooked chick peas. Stir well, cover, turn down heat to simmer and cook until the rice is tender and the liquid is absorbed — approx 20 minutes.

Turn off heat and allow to stand for further 10 minutes.

Serve the chick pea and rice mixture on a platter, garnished with the almonds and chicken pieces.

Chicken with Onions

Djaaj b'Bassal

Serves: 4-6
Cooking time: 1-1½ hours

½ cup ghee or substitute (see page 27)
1 large tender chicken
6 very small onions, peeled and left whole
1 tablespoon flour
6 cups boiling water
2 teaspoons salt
½ teaspoon black pepper
1 teaspoon mixed spices (see page 21)
½ cup lemon juice

Heat the ghee in a large frying pan, add the onions and chicken and cook until brown. Remove the onions and set aside and transfer the chicken to a large pot.

Drain the ghee from the frying pan, leaving just enough to brown the flour.

Brown the flour, stir in the boiling water and simmer for a few minutes. When the mixture is smooth pour it over the chicken. Add salt, pepper and spices. Cover and simmer on top of the stove or place in a 160°C (325°F) oven and cook as a casserole.

Add the fried onions half-way through cooking time, i.e. after about ½-¾ hour.

Stir in the lemon juice just before serving.

To serve, remove the onions and place them on a serving platter. Arrange the chicken pieces over the onions and pour some of the chicken juice over the top. Accompany with Rice Pilaf (see page 30).

Stuffed Roast Chicken

Djaaj Mihshi

Serves: 4
Cooking time: 1¾ hours

1 roasting chicken
2 cups Rice Stuffing for Poultry (see page 29)
½ cup ghee or substitute (see page 27)
1 cup water
½ teaspoon salt
1 tablespoon cornflour/cornstarch mixed to a paste with a little water

Prepare and stuff the chicken with rice stuffing as in the recipe for Stuffed Chicken and Soup (page 43).

Rub the stuffed chicken with ghee, wrap in aluminium foil and bake in moderate oven, 180-200°C (350-400°F) for 1¼ hours. Remove foil and continue to bake until tender and browned.

Make a gravy by heating the water, salt and ½ cup of the juice from the cooked chicken in a small saucepan. Stir in the cornflour/cornstarch paste just before the mixture comes to the boil and continue stirring until it thickens.

Cut the chicken into pieces and serve on a platter with the stuffing, accompanied by the gravy.

Stuffed Turkey

Habash Mihshi

Serves: 8-10
Cooking time: approx 20 minutes for each 500 g (1 lb) of turkey

1 turkey, approx 6-8 kg (13-17 lb)
4 cups Rice Stuffing for Poultry (see page 29)
water
2 tablespoons salt
2 cups yoghurt or 1 cup ghee (see page 27)

Remove the neck bone and stuff the turkey, including the neck skin, with the rice stuffing. Sew up the opening with coarse white thread.

Place the turkey in a large pot with enough water to barely cover. Add the salt, bring to the boil and skim. Cover and simmer gently until tender.

When cooked, remove the turkey from the pot and place in a roasting tray. Coat with yoghurt or ghee and brown in a hot oven. Remove cotton thread.

Slice turkey and serve on a platter together with stuffing.

KIBBI

Kibbi is the national dish of Lebanon. Basically a mixture of ground meat and bur'ghul (a crushed wheat, see page 20), it is extremely nourishing, yet economical, and can be used in a variety of ways — raw, baked, stuffed or with sauces.

The ideal meat for kibbi is a leg of mutton. Young lamb is unsuitable for most dishes as the meat is too tender and does not bind together well, however it may be used for *Kibbi Nayye* (kibbi eaten raw). As a last resort, ground lean topside beef may be substituted for mutton.

Nowadays in Lebanon the meat for kibbi can be bought already prepared from the butcher, but until recently the preparation was a time consuming ritual. The pounding of the meat in a stone or metal mortar (jorn) with a heavy pestle (madaqqa) was a long and tedious procedure. Today a fine bladed electric mincer or food processor is used.

We have included the full method of preparing kibbi meat (in the recipe for the Basic Kibbi Mixture), however if you want to save time you may find a Lebanese butcher from whom kibbi meat can be bought already prepared and ground. Alternatively, your local butcher might prepare the mutton leg for you if you give him enough notice and pay a little extra for his effort.

Moulding Basic Kibbi Mixture (page 56) into Kibbiyet and Or'rus shells (page 58).

Basic Kibbi Mixture

This recipe forms the basis of all kibbi dishes. As it is impossible to estimate exactly how much ground meat you will get from a leg of mutton, we have given only approximate measures for both it and the bur'ghul. When measuring these basic ingredients be sure to keep the proportions at 1½ cups of bur'ghul to every 500 g (1 lb) of ground meat. It is essential to keep the mixture cold while kneading and grinding.

Makes: 2.5 kg (5 lb) — enough to make 2-4 varieties of kibbi for 4-6 people

approx 4½ cups bur'ghul (see page 20)
1 leg of mutton to make approx 1.5 kg (3 lb) ground meat
3 medium onions
1 red pepper
1 tablespoon salt, or to taste
1 teaspoon freshly ground black pepper
1 teaspoon mixed spices (see page 21)
½ teaspoon cinnamon
iced water or ice

Wash the bur'ghul in cold water and drain well by taking handfuls and squeezing the water out. (It is a good idea to wash and drain the bur'ghul a few hours before making up this recipe. Keep it in the refrigerator until required.)

With a sharp knife remove the meat from the bone, then remove all the fat and gristle from the meat. Grind the lean meat twice through the fine blade of the mincer.

Grind the onions and red pepper and knead them into the meat together with the salt, pepper, mixed spices and cinnamon.

Knead the bur'ghul into the meat mixture, adding an occasional tablespoon of iced water or a small piece of ice to keep the mixture smooth and cold.

Put the kneaded mixture through the fine blade of the mincer twice. For the best results refrigerate in a covered container for 6-12 hours then knead again for a few minutes before cooking.

If you do not have a mincer: Buy finely ground meat and knead all the ingredients well together for about half an hour, constantly adding small amounts of iced water to keep the mixture cool and smooth. Refrigerate for a few hours and knead well again for about 15 minutes before cooking.

Variation:
For a hot spicier flavour, substitute ½-1 hot red pepper for the plain red pepper.

Kibbi Nayye
Kibbi Eaten Raw

When kibbi is to be eaten raw the proportion of bur'ghul to meat is generally reduced to 1 cup bur'ghul to every 500 g (1 lb) of ground meat, however the Basic Kibbi Mixture (see left) is a satisfactory alternative. Kibbi Nayye should always be eaten the same day—use any leftovers for cooked kibbi dishes.

Serves: 6-8

1 kg (2 lb) kibbi mixture

Make kibbi mixture as for basic recipe (see left).

Mould the mixture into oval shapes half the size of a small saucer, arrange on a serving platter and decorate with fresh mint.

This dish is generally served with a small jug of olive oil for pouring and is accompanied by a peeled and quartered raw onion, Hot Pepper and Onion Paste (see below) or Meat and Nut Filling (see page 29), and fresh bread. It may also be eaten plain or spread thickly on a slice of bread as an open sandwich.

Hot Pepper and Onion Paste
Titbeeleh Ⓥ Ⓛ

This paste is generally eaten with Kibbi Nayye.

Makes: ½ cup

1 medium onion
1 small hot red pepper
salt

Grind or blend all the ingredients together into a paste.

Kibbi b'Zait

Baked Kibbi in Oil

1 cup olive oil or substitute oil
1 kg (2 lb) Basic Kibbi Mixture (see left)

Grease a shallow edged baking dish, approx 30cm x 25cm (12in x 10in), with olive oil.

Place the mixture in the baking dish, pat and smooth down with wet hands until the tray is evenly covered with the mixture 1.5 cm (½ in) thick. Make deep horizontal or diagonal lines to form square or diamond shapes in the mixture so the oil can penetrate (see picture below).

Cover the mixture with a thick film of oil and bake on the centre shelf of the oven at 230°C (450°F) for approximately 20 minutes, then move to the top shelf for 10 minutes to brown the top.

This kibbi is delicious eaten hot or cold, wrapped in bread as a snack or accompanied by yoghurt and a fresh green salad.

Cutting diagonal shapes in Kibbi b'Zait to allow oil to penetrate.

Baked Stuffed Kibbi Loaf

Kibbi b'Tab'etain

Serves: 6-8
Cooking time: 1-1¼ hours

1 cup ghee or substitute (see page 27)
2 kg (4 lb) Basic Kibbi Mixture (see left)
3 cups Meat and Nut Filling (see page 29)

With a little of the ghee, thoroughly grease a 30 cm (12 in) square baking tray.

With wet hands smooth half the kibbi mixture into the tray, covering the bottom completely with a 1.5 cm (½ in) thickness.

Spread the filling evenly over the kibbi on the tray, then cover the filling with the remainder of the kibbi mixture to the same 1.5 cm (½ in) thickness. Cut deep horizontal or diagonal lines through both layers of the kibbi to form square or diamond shapes (see picture) so the ghee can penetrate.

Dot the remainder of the ghee on top of the kibbi in the tray and place in a moderate oven, 180-200°C (350-400°F), until golden brown on top — approximately 1-1¼ hours.

Serve hot or cold with stews, yoghurt or salads.

Kibbi Shells

Kibbiyet and Or'rus are shells moulded from the Basic Kibbi Mixture. Kibbiyet are long oval-shaped shells, filled or left hollow, which are baked or deep fried. Or'rus are pie-shaped shells, filled with hot shortening or meat filling, which are grilled.

Kibbiyet
Oval Kibbi Shells

Makes: 6-10 kibbiyet
Cooking time: 10-15 minutes

500 g (1 lb) Basic Kibbi Mixture (see page 56)
Meat and Nut Filling (see page 29) (optional)
olive or nut oil for frying, or ½ cup ghee or
    substitute (see page 27) for baking

With wet hands mould the kibbi mixture into balls a little larger than the size of a golf ball.

In turn hold each kibbi ball in your left hand and with the index finger of your right hand make a hole in it. Work the finger around the hole until a long thin shell is formed. The shell should be thin and smooth. Keep hands wet during the procedure and repair breaks in the shell with wet fingers.

Fill each shell with 2 teaspoons of Meat and Nut Filling or leave empty. Close the openings with wet fingers and smooth the shells into oval shapes or pat them back into round shapes.

Deep fry the shells in oil or bake them in ghee in an oven tray.

Or'rus
Pie-Shaped Kibbi Shells

Makes: 4-6 or'rus
Cooking time: 15-20 minutes

500 g (1 lb) Basic Kibbi Mixture (see page 56)
1½-2 cups Meat and Nut Filling (see page 29),
    or 1 cup solid butter, margarine or ground
    mutton fat
salt

With wet hands mould some of the kibbi mixture into a dish shape, about the size of a small saucer — approx 8 cm (3 in) in diameter. Lay the shell upside down over a small inverted soup bowl and make an identical shell (see picture, page 54).

Fill the second shell with Meat and Nut Filling or solid butter, margarine or ground mutton fat.

Place the first shell over the second shell to form a pie shape. With wet hands securely seal the rims of both shells together.

Repeat the above procedure until all the kibbi has been used.

Rub the top of each Or'rus with slightly salted water. Place under a very hot grill and cook until browned on top, turn over and brown underside.

Kibbi b'Zait (page 57), Kibbi Balls in Yoghurt (page 60) and Kibbiyet and Or'rus shells (above).

Kibbi Balls in Yoghurt

Lubb'neehey

When making this dish it is important to remember never to cover the yoghurt while cooking and always to stir it in the one direction to prevent curdling.

Serves: 8
Cooking time: 1 hour

1 cup Basic Kibbi Mixture (see page 56)
½ cup rice, washed and drained
2 cups water
3 cups yoghurt
1 egg white
1 teaspoon salt
lemon juice to taste (optional)

With wet hands, mould the kibbi mixture into small hollow balls about the size and shape of a small egg (see Kibbiyet directions, page 58).

Place the rice and water in a saucepan and bring quickly to the boil. Lower heat to simmer, cover, and cook until rice is nearly tender and most of the water is absorbed.

Beat together the yoghurt, egg white and salt. Add this mixture to the simmering rice and beat with egg beater. The mixture should have the consistency of thick soup. Add more water if necessary.

Bring the mixture back to the boil, stirring occasionally to prevent it sticking to the bottom of the pan. Stir in the kibbi balls gently and continue to boil for 5 minutes; lower heat and simmer for a further 5 minutes. Turn off the heat and cover saucepan. Allow to stand for 5 minutes before serving. If a more tart flavour is required, add lemon juice to taste before serving.

Kibbi Balls and Chick Peas in Tahini

Kibbi Arnabeeyeh

Serves: 6-8
Cooking time: 1½ hours

500 g (1 lb) Basic Kibbi Mixture (see page 56)
2 large onions, chopped in large pieces
½ cup ghee or substitute (see page 27)
500 g (1 lb) meat and bones for broth
  (preferably mutton)
water
1½ cups chick peas, soaked overnight (see page 20)
1½ cups tahini (see page 21)
½ cup lemon juice

With wet hands mould the kibbi mixture into small balls and place aside.

Brown the onions in the ghee and drain.

Cover the meat and bones with water and bring to the boil; skim fat from the top of the water. Add the drained, soaked chick peas and the browned onions. Simmer for 1½ hours, then remove the meat from the broth to prevent overcooking.

Bring the broth to the boil. Mix the tahini well with the lemon juice and pour into the boiling broth. Add the kibbi balls and continue to boil for 10 minutes.

Return meat to the broth, turn heat down and simmer slowly until the oil from the tahini floats to the top. Serve hot, accompanied by a bowl of Rice Pilaf (see page 30).

Kibbi Shishbarak

Kibbi Balls with Meat Pies and Yoghurt

Serves: 6-8
Cooking time: 1 hour 5 minutes

500 g (1 lb) Basic Kibbi Mixture (see page 56)
1½ cups plain flour
½ cup water
1 cup Meat and Nut Filling (see page 29)
1.25 litres (2 pints) Cooked Yoghurt (see page 28)

With wet hands mould the kibbi mixture into small balls about half the size of an egg.

Make the flour and water into a simple dough and roll out thinly. Using a biscuit cutter, cut into circles about 4 cm (1½ in) in diameter.

Place 1 teaspoonful of the Meat and Nut Filling on one side of each dough circle, then fold the other side of the circle over the top, pressing the ends together to form a crescent-shaped pie *(shishbarak)*.

Arrange the pies on a greased baking sheet and place them in a moderate oven long enough only to dry out the dough. Alternatively they can be dried out by exposing to the air.

Prepare the yoghurt and while it is simmering add the kibbi balls. After 10 minutes add the little pies and continue to simmer for a further 10-15 minutes.

Although not true kibbi dishes, the following fish and lenten recipes are based on the traditional kibbi meat bake, Kibbi b'Zait.

Fish Kibbi

Kibbit Sumak

Serves: 6-8
Cooking time: 35 minutes

1.5 kg (3 lb) jewfish or mackerel fillets
2 medium onions, finely ground
3 teaspoons salt
1 teaspoon white pepper
2 teaspoons ground coriander
2 tablespoons grated orange peel
1 cup finely chopped parsley
4 cups bur'ghul, washed and drained (see page 20)
¼ cup olive or nut oil
3 medium onions, cut into rings
½ cup pine nuts
¼ teaspoon powdered saffron

Skin the fish fillets and cut into small pieces. Finely grind them in a mincer.

Add the ground onions, salt, pepper, coriander, grated orange peel and chopped parsley. Mix well.

Gradually knead in the bur'ghul, adding a little ice during the process to help bind the mixture.

Put the mixture through the mincer.

Heat the oil in a large baking dish, about 35cm x 30cm (14in x 12in), and lightly sauté the onion rings and pine nuts.

Remove the pan from the heat, spread the onions and nuts evenly over the bottom and sprinkle with saffron.

Spread a layer of the mixture evenly over the onions to a thickness of approximately 1.25 cm (½ in). Cut through as in meat kibbi (see page 57).

Bake in a hot oven, 220°C (425°F), until golden brown — approx 30 minutes.

Serve hot with Spicy Rice for Fish (see page 49) or cold with salads.

Potato and Wheat Loaf

Kibbit Batorta Ⓥ Ⓛ

Serves: 8
Cooking time: 45-50 minutes

750 g (1½ lb) potatoes
2 large onions, ground or grated
1½ tablespoons salt
½ teaspoon black pepper
1 teaspoon ground cinnamon
1½ cups bur'ghul (see page 20)
1 cup plain flour
1 cup finely chopped parsley
¼ cup finely chopped mint
1½ cups olive or nut oil

Boil the potatoes in their jackets, peel and pound to a paste-like consistency with the ground or grated onion, salt, pepper and ground cinnamon. Knead in the bur'ghul, then the flour. Add the parsley and mint and knead again.

Bake in a baking dish with oil exactly as for Kibbi b'Zait (see page 57).

Serve cold, either by itself or with salad or bread.

MEAT

In the past meat was not always plentiful or of good quality. To overcome these problems it was either ground or cut into small pieces and cooked with cereals and vegetables to absorb the nutrients and flavour of the juices and to make the meat go further.

Although good quality meat is now readily available in Lebanon the popularity of the traditional meat recipes has not waned. They are generally made with lamb or mutton, but beef is a satisfactory substitute.

Lahem Mishwi (page 64) and Kafta on Skewers (page 65) with Lebanese Bread (page 31).

Lahem Mishwi

Meat on Skewers

Serves: 4-6
Cooking time: 10-15 minutes

1 kg (2 lb) tender lamb (preferably from the leg) or tender beef
½ cup olive oil or substitute
4 cloves crushed garlic
1 teaspoon mixed spices (see page 21)
salt and black pepper
4 onions, quartered and split
2 green peppers, cut into 2.5 cm (1 in) squares

Cut the meat into 2.5 cm (1 in) cubes, leaving a little fat on some pieces. Place the cubes in a bowl and mix in the oil, garlic, spices, salt and pepper. Refrigerate for one or two hours, but remove from refrigerator 1 hour before cooking.

Thread the meat, onion and green pepper pieces onto the skewers alternately. Barbecue or grill them, basting occasionally with the oil and garlic mixture left in the bowl. (If barbecuing, a handful of herbs is often thrown over the fire to give added aroma.)

As soon as the meat is cooked wrap an open piece of Lebanese bread around the meat to catch the juices and serve accompanied by Tahini Sauce (see page 26) and Tabbouleh or other salads (see page 88).

Variation:
The skewered meat and vegetables may be cooked plain, i.e. without oil or garlic.

Bur'ghul b'Lahem

Bur'ghul and Meat

This dish is equally delicious when cooked with chicken instead of meat.

Serves: 4-6
Cooking time: 2 hours 50 minutes

2 cups bur'ghul (see page 20)
3 medium onions, finely chopped
1 cup ghee or substitute (see page 27)
750 g (1½ lb) lean stewing meat, cubed
3 teaspoons salt
¼ teaspoon black pepper
1 teaspoon mixed spices (see page 21)
3 tomatoes, peeled
4 tablespoons tomato paste

Wash and drain the bur'ghul by squeezing with cupped hands. Set aside for at least half an hour.

In a frying pan fry the onions in half the ghee until soft, add the meat and fry for a few minutes until lightly browned. Season with salt, pepper and spices.

Place the meat and onions in a casserole dish. Add the peeled tomatoes, tomato paste and enough water to cover the meat. Cover and bake in a moderate oven until meat is tender — approx 2 hours.

When cooked, drain the sauce off the meat and measure 3 cups back into the casserole dish. Bring to the boil.

Add the remaining ghee to the frying pan and gently fry the dry bur'ghul for 10 minutes, stirring constantly.

Place the bur'ghul in the casserole dish, spreading it evenly over the boiling meat and sauce. Cover and bake in a moderate oven for 30 minutes. It is cooked when the liquid is absorbed and the bur'ghul is moist and fluffy. If the liquid is absorbed before the bur'ghul is cooked, add a little more boiling sauce or water and return to the oven.

Basic Kafta Mixture

Kafta mixture is basically finely ground meat, but unlike kibbi it is not made up entirely of lean meat. Kafta may be made from either lamb or beef. Ordinary hamburger ground meat is also quite satisfactory.

Makes: 1 kg (2 lb)

1 kg (2 lb) finely ground beef, lamb or hamburger meat
1 cup finely chopped parsley
1 teaspoon mixed spices (see page 21)
1 cup finely chopped or ground onions
3 teaspoons salt
½ teaspoon black pepper

Mix all the ingredients together in a large bowl and knead well.

Place the mixture through the fine blade of a grinder twice or alternatively knead well for a further 20 minutes, occasionally adding small quantities of iced water.

Kafta on Skewers

Kafta Mishweeyeh b'Sseekh

Serves: 4-6
Cooking time: 10-15 minutes

1 kg (2 lb) Basic Kafta Mixture (see above)

With wet fingers, mould the kafta mixture into meat balls slightly larger than an egg. Thread a skewer through each meat ball and mould the meat into a finger shape along the skewers.

Gently barbecue or grill the meat, making sure not to overcook as it will dry out.

When cooked, remove the meat from the skewers with open pieces of Lebanese bread, which are then left around the meat to make juicy sandwiches. The sandwiches are usually accompanied by Hoummus b'Tahini (see page 34). If preferred, the kafta may be served without bread but accompanied by a salad.

Kafta Meat Loaf

Kafta b'Ssaineeyeh

Serves: 4-6
Cooking time: 40 minutes

1 kg (2 lb) Basic Kafta Mixture (see left)
3 tablespoons tomato paste
1 cup water

Spread the kafta mixture evenly over a large baking tray, approx 30cm x 25cm (12in x 10in) and 2.5cm (1 in) thick. Bake in a moderate oven until lightly browned — approx 10 minutes.

Mix the tomato paste with the water, pour over the meat in the tray and continue baking until half the juice is absorbed into the meat — approx 20 minutes.

Remove the tray from the oven, place on a hotplate and keep at moderate heat until most of the juice is absorbed into the meat — approx 10 minutes.

Cut into squares and serve hot with mashed potatoes and cooked vegetables.

Mi'leeyeh

Fried Meat Patties

Serves: 4-6
Cooking time: 15-20 minutes

1 egg white
1 kg (2 lb) Basic Kafta Mixture (see left)
flour
olive or nut oil

Mix the unbeaten egg white into the kafta mixture. Mould the mixture into little patties. Dip the patties in flour and pan-fry in hot oil.

Serve with potato chips and salad or sautéed vegetables. Hoummus b'Tahini (see page 34) can be used as a sauce.

Dawood Baasha

Meatballs and Pine Nuts in Tomato Sauce

Serves: 6
Cooking time: 40 minutes

½ kg (1 lb) **Basic Kafta Mixture, omitting**
  parsley (see page 65)
1 cup pine nuts
½ cup olive or nut oil
2 large onions, chopped
4 medium tomatoes, peeled
2 tablespoons tomato paste blended with
  1 cup water
½ teaspoon mixed spices (see page 21)
salt and black pepper
juice of half a lemon

Mould the kafta mixture into balls about half the
size of an egg.

In a saucepan lightly brown the pine nuts in oil,
remove and set aside. Fry the onions in the same oil
until golden brown, remove and set aside, then
brown the meat balls and set aside.

Place the peeled tomatoes and tomato paste
blended with water in the pan and bring to the boil.
Add the mixed spices, salt and pepper, lemon juice,
onions and meat balls. Simmer for 20 minutes
adding a little more water if required. Add the pine
nuts just before serving.

Serve with Rice Pilaf (see page 30).

Lentils with Meat

M'judra b'Lahem

Serves: 4-6
Cooking Time: 1 hour

500 g (1 lb) coarsely ground meat, preferably
  mutton or lamb
1 tablespoon ghee or substitute (see page 27)
1 medium onion, finely chopped
1 cup brown lentils, prepared and washed
  (see page 21)
5 cups water
1 cup rice, washed and drained
1½ teaspoons salt
½ teaspoon black pepper

Lightly brown the meat in the hot ghee, add the
onion and cook until transparent — approx 10
minutes.

Boil the lentils in the water until tender. Drain
the water off the lentils and measure 2 cups back
into the saucepan. If necessary add more water to
make up the quantity.

Bring the lentils back to the boil. Stir in the rice,
meat and onions, salt and pepper. Allow the
mixture to bubble for a few seconds, turn down to
simmer, cover tightly, and cook until all the water is
absorbed — approx 15 minutes.

Adjust salt and pepper to taste.

Baked Macaroni with Meat

Ma'karoni b'Ssaneeyeh

Serves: 6
Cooking time: 1 hour

375 g (12 oz) macaroni pasta
2 large onions, finely chopped
¼ cup ghee or substitute (see page 27)
500 g (1 lb) coarsely ground meat
2 teaspoons salt
½ teaspoon pepper
½ teaspoon mixed spices (see page 21)
¼ teaspoon ground cinnamon
1 tablespoon vinegar
4 tablespoons tomato paste
1 cup tomato juice or canned tomato soup
½ cup water
4 eggs (optional)
½ cup grated cheese

Cook the macaroni in boiling salted water until tender. Drain, rinse in cold water, drain again and set aside.

Sauté the onions in the ghee, add the meat and cook until brown all over — approximately 10 minutes. Add the salt, pepper, mixed spices and cinnamon, then stir in the vinegar, tomato paste, tomato juice or soup and the water. Cover and simmer gently until meat is tender — 30–35 minutes.

Spread half the cooked macaroni in an even layer over the bottom of a casserole dish. Pour the meat mixture evenly over it, then cover in an even layer with the remaining macaroni.

Beat the eggs and pour over the top of the macaroni, allowing it to seep through the entire mixture.

Bake in a moderately hot oven, 200°C (400°F), for 40 minutes. Remove from oven and while still hot, sprinkle with grated cheese. Serve warm.

Ghammee

Stuffed Tripe

As this recipe takes several hours to make, it is generally prepared the day before it is cooked.

Serves: 7
Cooking time: 4 hours

1.5 kg (3 lb) tripe
1 tablespoon salt
4 litres (6 pints) cold water
1 cinnamon stick
Stuffing:
750 g (1½ lb) ground meat with fat
500 g (1 lb) small whole onions or quartered large onions
2 teaspoons salt
1 teaspoon mixed spices (see page 21)
1 teaspoon black pepper
¼ teaspoon powdered saffron
1½ cups rice
½ cup chick peas, soaked overnight (see page 20) and cracked with rolling pin
¼ cup water

Mix all stuffing ingredients together and set aside.

Wash the tripe and cut into seven pieces. Place the pieces in boiling water for 1 minute. Wash again in cold water, then rub inside and outside with ½ tablespoon salt.

With coarse cotton thread sew the sides of each piece of tripe into a little sack. Fill each sack with stuffing, sew up the opening.

Place the stuffed tripe sacks in a large pot with the water, remaining salt and cinnamon stick. Bring to the boil, skim the surface, reduce heat and simmer until tender — approx 4 hours.

When cooked, remove cotton thread and cinnamon stick. Chop up tripe and mix it with stuffing before serving. Alternatively, cut each bag into three slices.

Serve the tripe at the same time as the broth, but in separate bowls.

STEWS

Stews have been popular in the Middle East, as in most other parts of the world, since the earliest times. In Bagdad recipes dating as far back as 1226 have been found.

In the past stews were always simmered very slowly in a heavy pot on top of a stove or open fire. Today they can be cooked successfully in a covered pot in the oven or in an electric slow cooker, however pressure cooking does not give good results.

The best meat to use for these stews is mutton, but any type of stewing meat may be substituted. They are generally accompanied by Rice Pilaf or Bur'ghul Pilaf (see page 30).

Okra Stew (page 71) accompanied by Rice Pilaf (page 30).

Green Bean Stew
Yakh'nit Loobyeh

Serves: 6
Cooking time: 2½ hours

500 g (1 lb) fresh green string beans
500 g (1 lb) stewing meat, cubed
several meat bones
1½ cups onions, chopped
½ cup ghee or substitute (see page 27)
1½ teaspoons salt
½ teaspoon pepper
½ teaspoon mixed spices (see page 21)
2 tablespoons tomato paste blended with 2½
  cups water or 1 x 445 g (15 oz) can tomato
  soup blended with 2 cups water
2 cloves garlic
1 teaspoon ground coriander

String the beans. Slice down the centre or leave whole.

Lightly brown the meat, bones and onions in the ghee, using the pot in which the stew is to be cooked. Mix in the beans and fry for a few minutes. Add the salt, pepper and mixed spices, then pour in the tomato paste or soup diluted with water. Bring to the boil, cover and simmer slowly until the meat is very tender.

Crush the garlic with a pinch of salt and fry with the coriander in a little ghee until the garlic smells sweet. Stir this mixture into the cooked stew.

Serve with Rice Pilaf or Bur'ghul Pilaf (see page 30).

Variation:
Substitute peas for beans to make Green Pea Stew.

Dried Bean Stew
Yakh'nit Fassoulia

Serves: 4
Cooking time: 3½ hours

2 cups dried white beans, soaked overnight (see
  page 20)
2 large onions, finely chopped
2-3 cloves garlic, crushed
500 g (1 lb) stewing meat, cubed
¼ cup ghee or substitute (see page 27)
2 large tomatoes, peeled and chopped
4 tablespoons tomato paste
2½ teaspoons salt
½ teaspoon black pepper
½ teaspoon mixed spices (see page 21)
water

Drain the beans and place in a large saucepan. Cover well with water and bring to the boil, turn down heat and simmer until tender. Drain and set aside.

Lightly brown the onions, garlic and meat in the ghee. Add tomatoes, tomato paste, salt, pepper and spices. Sauté gently for a few minutes. Stir in the cooked beans.

Pour over enough water to *just* cover. Bring to the boil, turn down the heat, cover and simmer until the meat is very tender or cook as a casserole in a moderate oven for 2-2½ hours. Adjust salt and pepper to taste.

Serve with Rice or Bur'ghul Pilaf (see page 30).

Spinach Stew
Yakh'nit Spanneegh

Serves: 4-6
Cooking time: 1¼ hours

1 cup chick peas, soaked overnight (see page 20)
500 g (1 lb) **Basic Kafta Mixture** (see page 65)
2 tablespoons ghee or substitute (see page 27)
500 g (1 lb) spinach
1 teaspoon salt
½ teaspoon black pepper
2 cloves garlic
1 teaspoon ground coriander

Boil the chick peas, cover and simmer until tender. Drain and set aside.

Make small balls with the kafta mixture. Brown them lightly in the ghee, using the saucepan in which the stew is to be cooked. Remove from saucepan and set aside.

Place the spinach in the saucepan, cover and simmer gently in its own juice until tender. Add meat balls, chick peas, ½ teaspoon salt and the pepper. Cover and continue to simmer (adding a little water when necessary) until the meat balls are well cooked — approx ½ hour.

At the completion of cooking, crush the remainder of the salt with the garlic, add the coriander and fry in a little ghee until the garlic smells sweet. Mix this mixture into the cooked stew. Adjust salt to taste.

Serve with Rice Pilaf (see page 30).

Okra Stew
Yakh'nit Bameh

Serves: 6
Cooking time: 1½-1¾ hours

500 g (1 lb) fresh okra or 1 x 800 g (28 oz) can
500 g (1 lb) stewing meat, cubed
1 large onion, chopped
½ cup ghee or substitute (see page 27)
2 ripe medium tomatoes, peeled and sliced
1½ teaspoons salt
½ teaspoon black pepper
½ teaspoon mixed spices (see page 21)
3 tablespoons tomato paste blended with
    2 cups water
2 cloves garlic
1 teaspoon ground coriander
2 tablespoons lemon juice

Wash the fresh okra (see below for canned okra) and cut off the stems.

Lightly brown the meat and onion in ghee, using the pot in which the stew is to be cooked. Add the fresh okra and fry gently for a few minutes.

Mix in the tomatoes and simmer for a few more minutes. Season with salt, pepper and mixed spices. Add the tomato paste diluted with water.

Bring to the boil, cover and simmer slowly until meat is tender, adding more water if necessary.

Crush the garlic with a little salt and fry with the coriander in 1 tablespoon of ghee until the garlic smells sweet. Stir this mixture into the cooked stew and add the lemon juice.

If using canned okra: Make the stew as directed but do not add the okra until the meat is tender. Add the juice with the okra and continue to simmer uncovered for approximately 5-10 minutes. If canned okra already has tomato juice, omit the 3 tablespoons of tomato paste from the recipe.

Darweesh Rosary
Mas'bahet ed'Darweesh

Serves: 4
Cooking time: 2 hours

½ cup ghee or substitute (see page 27)
2 medium onions, chopped
2 cloves garlic, crushed
500 g (1 lb) stewing meat, cubed
1 large eggplant, peeled, cubed and prepared
    for cooking (see page 20)
1 large potato, sliced
5 medium tomatoes, peeled and chopped
1 teaspoon salt
¼ teaspoon pepper
½ teaspoon mixed spices (see page 21)

In the hot ghee, brown the onions, garlic, meat, eggplant, potato and tomatoes. Add salt, pepper, spices and enough water to cover. Pour into a baking pan and bake in a moderate oven, 180°C (350°F), stirring at intervals, until meat and vegetables are tender — approx 1¾ hours.

When the vegetables and meat are cooked, remove to top of stove and simmer uncovered until excess sauce evaporates. Adjust salt and pepper to taste.

Serve hot.

Meat and Yoghurt Stew
Lubban Oummu

Serves: 8
Cooking time: 1½ hours

1 kg (2 lb) stewing meat (preferably lamb) cut
    into large pieces
8 small whole white onions, peeled, or
    2 medium onions, quartered
2 teaspoons salt
½ teaspoon pepper
1 cinnamon stick
2½ cups Cooked Yoghurt, omitting garlic (see
    page 28)
2 cloves garlic
1 tablespoon ghee or substitute (see page 27)
1 teaspoon ground coriander

Place the meat and onions in a saucepan, add salt, pepper and cinnamon stick. Cover with water, bring to the boil, cover and simmer until the meat is very tender and most of the water has been evaporated. If too much water is left after the meat is cooked, drain some of it off. Remove cinnamon stick.

Bring the yoghurt to the boil and, stirring well, add it to the cooked meat and onions while they are still simmering. Continue to simmer this mixture uncovered for 15 minutes.

Crush the garlic with a little salt. Fry it in ghee with the coriander until the garlic smells sweet. Stir this mixture into the cooked stew. Adjust seasoning to taste.

Serve hot with Rice Pilaf or Bur'ghul Pilaf (see page 30).

LENTEN DISHES

Out of necessity often has come the creation of some of the world's most outstanding cuisine. In Lebanon this is true of the country's famous lenten dishes.

Until modern times only stored grain and dried vegetables were available for food in the mountain areas during the cold winters. This factor, together with the country's religious background which forbids the eating of meat, eggs or milk foods during Lent and other religious periods, resulted in the origination of many meat and dairy free recipes.

Some lenten recipes are hundreds of years old. *Fool m'Dammas*, for example, dates back to at least the Middle Ages. It was originally known as "poor man's food", but is today one of the most popular dishes in Lebanon.

Satisfying and nutritious, lenten dishes are ideal for vegetarians and those who like to limit their intake of meat, but they also make delicious accompaniments for meat-based meals.

This chapter contains recipes for the basic lenten dishes. Further lenten recipes are included in other chapters and can be readily identified by the symbol Ⓛ .

Endive Leaves in Oil (page 74), Lentil and Rice Pilaf (page 75) and Bread Cloth (page 31).

Fool m'Dammas
Dried Beans in Lemon Juice Ⓥ Ⓛ

Serves: 4
Cooking time: 45 minutes

500 g (1 lb) small dried broad/fava beans, soaked overnight (see page 20)
2 cloves garlic, crushed
½ cup olive oil
juice of 1 lemon
1 teaspoon salt
¼ teaspoon black pepper

Drain the beans and place in a large saucepan. Cover well with water, bring to the boil. Cover, turn down heat and simmer, adding more water and stirring when necessary, until the beans are tender — approx ¾ hour.

Drain the beans and mix in the crushed garlic, olive oil, lemon juice, salt and pepper.

Serve hot or cold.

Dried Beans with Onions
Fassoolia Humra Ⓥ Ⓛ

Borlotti and salluggia beans can be purchased from most health food stores and many delicatessens and supermarkets.

Serves: 4-6
Cooking time: 2½ hours

2 cups borlotti or salluggia beans, soaked overnight (see page 20)
2 large onions, chopped finely
¾ cup olive oil
2 teaspoons salt
½ teaspoon black pepper
1 teaspoon mixed spices (see page 21)
4 cups water
1 teaspoon dried mint

Drain beans.

In a large saucepan fry the onions in half the oil until very dark brown. Add the remainder of oil, the beans, salt, pepper and mixed spices. Sauté for a few minutes. Mix in the water, bring to the boil and boil vigorously for 10 minutes. Turn down the heat, cover tightly and simmer, stirring regularly and adding more water if necessary, until the beans are tender and the fluid is reduced — approx 1½-2½ hours.

If the fluid is not reduced when the beans have become tender, boil vigorously with the cover off until it does reduce. Mix in the dried mint.

Serve hot or cold.

Falafel
Spicy Dried Bean Patties Ⓥ Ⓛ

Makes: 35 patties
Cooking time: 5 minutes per batch

375 g (½ lb) broad/fava beans, soaked overnight (see page 20)
375 g (½ lb) chick peas, soaked overnight (see page 20)
2 cloves garlic, crushed
1 large brown onion, finely chopped
4 large spring onions, finely chopped
½ hot red or green pepper, finely chopped or ground
1 level tablespoon bicarbonate of soda
3 tablespoons plain flour
1 cup finely chopped parsley
1 teaspoon ground coriander
1–1½ teaspoons cumin
1½ tablespoons salt
½ teaspoon black pepper
oil for frying

Drain the beans and chick peas and rinse well in cold water. If the beans are not skinless, skin them. Pound or grind the beans and chick peas (if grinding, put them through the fine blade of the mincer twice). Mix in the crushed garlic, chopped onions, spring onions and hot pepper, then add the remaining ingredients. Pound or blend the mixture to a smooth paste and let rest for at least one hour.

Take walnut-sized lumps of the mixture and mould into round flat shapes 4 cm (1½ in) in diameter. Allow to rest for a further 15 minutes, then deep fry them in oil until golden brown.

Serve hot accompanied by a tomato and cucumber salad and Tahini Sauce (see page 26).

Variation:
Roll the round shapes of mixture in sesame seeds before frying.

Endive Leaves in Oil
Hindbeh b'Zait Ⓥ Ⓛ

Serves: 6
Cooking time: ½-1 hour

1 large bunch endives (approx size of a large lettuce)
2 large onions, chopped
¾ cup olive oil
salt

Wash and chop the endive leaves, then boil in a large pot of boiling water until tender — approx ½-1 hour. Drain and squeeze excess water out of the leaves with the palms of the hands, forming large balls. Undo the balls, and spread on a platter.

Fry the onions in the oil until golden. Remove half the onions and set aside.

Add the endive leaves and salt to the onions and oil in the pan and sauté for 10 minutes, stirring constantly. Turn out onto a platter and cover with the remaining onions. Serve hot or cold with bread or in a sandwich.

Green Beans in Oil
Loob'yeh b'Zait Ⓥ Ⓛ

Serves: 4-6
Cooking time: 50 minutes
500 g (1 lb) fresh green string beans
¾ cup olive oil
2 medium brown onions, finely chopped
1 teaspoon salt
½ teaspoon black pepper
1-2 cups water

String and slice the beans lengthwise.

Heat the olive oil in a saucepan and fry the onions until they are reddish-brown. Mix in the beans, salt and pepper. Sauté for 10 minutes.

Stir in the water, cover and simmer very slowly, adding more water if necessary, until the beans are very soft. Remove lid and continue to simmer uncovered to absorb excess juice — approx 10 minutes.

When cooked the beans should be very brown and soft. Adjust salt and pepper to taste.

To eat these beans the Lebanese way, hold a fork in one hand and push portions onto small pieces of Lebanese bread held in the other hand.

Variations:
• Add 2 medium sized peeled and chopped tomatoes to the raw beans.
• Substitute 1½ cups of fresh or canned tomato juice for the water.

Okra in Oil
Bameh b'Zait Ⓥ Ⓛ

Serves: 4
Cooking time: approx 1½ hours for fresh okra,
½ hour for canned okra
1 kg (2 lb) fresh young okra or 1 x 875 g (28 oz) can
of okra with liquid
¼ cup olive oil
12 very small white onions, peeled and left whole
2-3 cloves garlic, halved
500 g (1 lb) tomatoes, skinned and sliced

2 teaspoons salt
¼ teaspoon black pepper
½ cup water
1 lemon

Remove stems from the fresh okra.

Wash and dry the okra, then fry in the oil in a saucepan until lightly brown. Remove and set aside on absorbent paper.

Fry the onions and garlic in the same oil until slightly brown. Return the okra to the saucepan and add the tomatoes, salt, pepper and water. Stirring gently, bring to the boil. Cover tightly, turn down the heat and simmer very slowly until okra are tender — approx ¾-1 hour for fresh okra but much less for the canned variety.

When okra are tender, squeeze in the lemon juice and continue to simmer for a further 5 minutes. Adjust salt and pepper to taste.

Serve hot, or allow to cool in the saucepan and serve cold, with bread or Rice Pilaf (see page 30).

Lentil and Rice Pilaf
M'judra Byda Ⓥ Ⓛ

Serves: 6-8
Cooking time: 1 hour
1¾ cups lentils
2 large onions
1 cup olive or nut oil
6 cups water
2 cups rice, washed and drained
1 tablespoon salt

Prepare and wash lentils as directed on page 21.

Slice onions very finely into half circles, place in frypan with hot oil and fry until golden brown. Remove half the onions from the pan and place on absorbent paper to drain and crispen. Leave the remaining onions in the pan.

Boil the lentils in the water until nearly tender — approx 20-25 minutes. Mix in the rice and bring back to the boil.

Reheat the remaining onions and oil in the frypan until very hot. Pour them, with the oil, onto the boiling lentils and rice. Add salt, cover tightly, turn down the heat and simmer slowly until the rice is tender and all the fluid is absorbed — approx 20 minutes.

Serve hot or cold, garnished with the crisp brown onion slices. If served cold, accompany with a tossed salad.

STUFFED VEGETABLES

Stuffed vegetables are very popular throughout the Middle East and each country has developed its own variations. They are known as *dolma* in Turkey, *domathes* in Greece, *dolmeh* in Persia and *mihshi* in the Arab lands.

In Lebanon mihshi dishes are made with both meat and lenten fillings. We have given the traditional recipes for each vegetable. However, they often vary slightly from season to season and from town to town. The ideal size for zucchini and eggplant for stuffing is approximately 10–15 cm (4–6 in) long and 4–5 cm (1½–2 in) in diameter.

Mihshi are generally served with a variety of other dishes as part of the main course, but they may also be served as a meal in themselves. The usual accompaniments are bread and salad, and sometimes kibbi or yoghurt.

Stuffed Zucchini in Tomato Sauce (page 79).

TO COOK STUFFED VEGETABLES

When the stuffed vegetables have been packed tightly in the saucepan as directed in the individual recipes, take a heatproof plate and turn it upside-down over the top of the vegetables, pressing down firmly. Add enough water to cover the plate while it is under pressure.

Leave the plate in place and cover the saucepan securely. Bring quickly to the boil, turn down heat and simmer very slowly until the vegetables and stuffings are tender and the liquid has reduced and thickened. For maximum flavour leave the vegetables to cool in the saucepan with the juices. Reheat before serving.

To serve, drain the juice from the saucepan. Turn the stuffed vegetables onto a large platter and pour the juice over the top.

Cabbage Rolls

Mihshi Malfouf

Serves: 6
Cooking time: 1½ hours

1 medium cabbage
1 large onion, chopped (optional)
several lean meat bones for bottom of saucepan (optional)
1 tablespoon ghee (see page 27)
5 cloves garlic
4 cups Meat and Rice Stuffing (see page 29)
1½ tablespoons salt
½ cup lemon juice
1 teaspoon dried mint
water as required (see above)

Remove the core from the cabbage, separate and wash leaves. Dip them into boiling water a few at a time until they become wilted and pliable. Trim the large central veins flat (removing them if they are too hard to roll). Cut very large leaves in half but leave small ones whole.

Lightly brown the onion and bones in ghee using the saucepan in which the cabbage rolls are to be cooked. Drain off the ghee but leave the onion and bones in the bottom of the saucepan and add 3 cloves of garlic. Cover with one layer of cabbage leaves.

Take one of the remaining cabbage leaves at a time, lay it down with the inside up and place a tablespoonful of stuffing in the centre. Fold the bottom of the leaf over the stuffing, then roll tightly, forming a roll about 10-15 cm (4-6 in) long and 2.5-4 cm (1-1½ in) wide.

Pack the rolls, open ends down, in tight rows and layers in the saucepan, on top of the cabbage leaves covering the onions and bones. Sprinkle each layer with salt and lemon juice. Crush the remainder of the garlic, mix with the remainder of lemon juice and pour over the last layer of rolls. Sprinkle with mint.

Cook as directed at left.

Variation:
Dispense with the onion and meat bones and pack rolls directly over a layer of thick cabbage leaves.

Stuffed Grape Vine Leaves

Mihshi Warra Enib

Serves: 6
Cooking time: 1½ hours

1 medium brown onion, chopped (optional)
several lean meat bones, for bottom of saucepan (optional)
1 tablespoon ghee or substitute (see page 27)
3 cloves garlic
500 kg (1 lb) fresh, tender grape vine leaves
4 cups Meat and Rice Stuffing (see page 29)
1½ teaspoons salt
½ cup lemon juice
1 teaspoon dried mint
water as required (see above left)

Lightly brown the onion and meat bones in the ghee using the saucepan in which the vine leaves are to be cooked. Drain off the ghee but leave the onion and bones in the bottom of the saucepan and add 2 cloves of garlic. Cover with a layer of vine leaves.

Soften the remaining vine leaves by dipping a few at a time in boiling water. Taking one leaf at a time, lay it down with the rough side up and place a teaspoonful of stuffing in the centre. Fold the bottom of the leaf over the stuffing, then fold it in from each side to the middle. Roll tightly, forming a roll about 7.5-10 cm (3-4 in) long and 1.25-2.5 cm (½-1 in) thick.

Pack the rolls, open ends down, in tight rows and layers in the saucepan, on top of the layer of leaves covering the bones and onions. Sprinkle each layer with salt and lemon juice. Crush the remaining garlic clove, mix it with the remainder of the lemon juice and pour over the last layer of rolls. Sprinkle with mint.

Cook as directed above left.

Variations:
• Add one finely chopped tomato to the stuffing and include 2 medium sized sliced tomatoes in the bottom of the saucepan before cooking.
• Dispense with the onion and meat bones and pack rolls directly over a layer of leaves.

Stuffed Spinach Leaves

Warra Mihshi Sil'ih Ⓥ Ⓛ

This recipe requires only the spinach leaves. Use the stalks for the salad recipe on page 89.

Serves: 6
Cooking time: 1 hour

1.5 kg (3 lb) fresh spinach
4 cups Lenten Stuffing (see page 29)
2 tomatoes, sliced
2 cloves garlic
¼ cup lemon juice
1½ teaspoons salt

Remove the stalks from the spinach.

Soften the spinach leaves by dipping in boiling water. Cut into sections approximately 10 cm (4 in) square.

Place 2 teaspoons of stuffing on each spinach square. Roll up from the bottom and turn in the sides to form a roll approx 6 cm (2½ in) long.

Place the tomato slices and garlic cloves in a layer on the bottom of the saucepan. Add the spinach rolls in tightly packed rows and layers, with open ends down. Sprinkle each layer with lemon juice and salt.

Cook as directed at left.

Variation:
Grape vine leaves can be used instead of spinach.

Stuffed Tomatoes

Mihshi Banadoura

Serves: 3-6
Cooking time: 1 hour

6 large firm tomatoes
2 cups Meat and Nut Filling (see page 29)
1 tablespoon tomato paste
1 teaspoon salt
black pepper
2 tablespoons ghee

Wash the tomatoes and cut a thin slice off the top of each one. Scoop out the pulp and set aside.

Fill the tomatoes with the filling, replace the tops and arrange close together on a baking dish.

Sieve the tomato pulp and mix in the tomato paste, salt and pepper. Pour over the tomatoes. Dob each tomato with butter and bake in a pre-heated moderate oven until tomatoes are very soft — approximately ½ hour.

Serve with Rice Pilaf or Bur'ghul Pilaf (see page 30) as a main dish, or alternatively serve as an accompanying vegetable.

Stuffed Zucchini in Tomato Sauce

Mihshi Kousa b'Banadoura

The zucchini pulp is not required for this recipe. Use it for Zucchini and Egg Fritters (see page 85) or to enrich soups and stews.

Serves: 6
Cooking time: 1½ hours

18 small or 12 medium zucchini
4 cups Meat and Rice Stuffing (see page 29)
2 medium onions, chopped finely
4-5 tablespoons ghee or substitute (see page 27)
2-4 cloves garlic
2 tomatoes, sliced
1½ teaspoons salt
2 tablespoons tomato paste or 1 x 455 g (14½ oz) can tomatoes
4 cups water
1 teaspoon dried mint

Wash the zucchini and cut off the tops, just below the stems. Scoop out the pulp (see page 21) being careful not to break the skin: the other end must remain closed.

Rinse and drain the hollow zucchini. Three-quarters fill each one with stuffing, allowing for rice expansion.

Lightly brown the onions in the ghee using the saucepan in which the zucchini are to be cooked. Add the garlic and sliced tomatoes to the onions and ghee, covering the bottom of the saucepan evenly. Place the zucchini over the tomatoes, in closely packed rows and layers, sprinkling salt between each layer.

Mix the tomato paste or soup with the water and pour over the zucchini. Sprinkle with mint.

Turn a heatproof dinner plate upside-down over the zucchini to keep them in place and keep in the steam. Cover the saucepan. Bring to the boil, turn down the heat and simmer very slowly until the zucchini shells are tender and the filling cooked — approx 1-1½ hours.

When cooked, keep the zucchini covered and allow to cool in the juice. Reheat before serving.

To serve, drain the juice from the saucepan into another container. Gently place the zucchini on a platter and pour the juice over the top. Serve as a complete meal with side salad and bread.

Variations:
• For a richer flavour, some bones and a few pieces of stewing meat may be browned with the onions and left in the bottom of the saucepan to cook with the zucchini.
• The zucchini may be replaced by eggplant of the same size. This dish is called *Batinjaan Mihshi*.
• The zucchini may be replaced by chokos.

Stuffed Zucchini in Yoghurt Sauce

Mihshi Kousa b'Lubban

Serves: 4-6
Cooking time: 1½ hours

18 small or 12 medium zucchini
4 cups Meat and Rice Stuffing (see page 29)
1½ teaspoons salt, or to taste
1 cup water
1 litre (2¼ pints) Cooked Yoghurt (see page 28)
1-2 teaspoons dried mint

Prepare, scoop and stuff the zucchini as in Stuffed Zucchini in Tomato Sauce recipe (see page 79).

Place the zucchini in tight rows and layers in a saucepan, sprinkling salt over each layer. Add the water and bring to the boil. Cover, turn down the heat to very low, and simmer slowly until the zucchini are tender and the filling cooked, adding a little more water if required.

When the zucchini are cooked, bring the yoghurt to the boil and pour over the zucchini. Keeping the saucepan uncovered, bring the mixture back to the boil and allow to simmer vigorously for 15 minutes, shaking the saucepan from time to time to allow the sauce to penetrate.

When cooked, sprinkle with mint and turn off heat. Cover and allow to stand for at least half an hour before serving.

Serve as in recipe for Stuffed Zucchini in Tomato Sauce (see page 79).

Sheikh El Mihshi

Stuffed, Fried and Baked Eggplant

Serves: 4-6
Cooking time: 1 hour 20 minutes

14 small or 8 medium eggplants
¾ cup ghee or substitute (see page 27)
4 cups Meat and Nut Filling (see page 29)
1½ cups tomato juice or 1 tablespoon tomato paste
  blended with 1½ cups water

Clean eggplant and trim stems to about 1.25 cm (½ in). Do not remove hulls. Partially peel, leaving lengthwise strips of alternating peel and flesh.

Fry eggplant in ghee until soft, drain.

Slit each eggplant lengthwise to form a pocket. Gently press several spoonfuls of filling into the slits. Place in a casserole dish. Pour the tomato juice over the top, sprinkle with salt and pepper.

Cover and simmer on top of the stove for 15 minutes and then bake uncovered for 15 minutes in a hot oven to brown the tops.

Serve hot in the casserole dish, accompanied by Rice Pilaf or Bur'ghul Pilaf (see page 30).

Stuffed Eggplant

Mihshi Batinjaan Orteh Ⓥ Ⓛ

Serves: 4-6
Cooking time: 1¼ hours

12 very small eggplants
4 cups Lenten Stuffing (see page 29)
½ cup water
¼ cup olive or nut oil
4 large tomatoes, sliced finely
2 cloves garlic
salt

Scoop out the eggplants as with Stuffed Zucchini in Tomato Sauce (see page 79) and soak the shell in salted water (see page 20).

Moisten the stuffing with ½ cup water. Three-quarters fill the eggplants, allowing for rice expansion.

Heat the oil in a large saucepan. Place half the sliced tomatoes together with the garlic in layers in the bottom of the saucepan. Closely pack the eggplants in layers over the tomatoes. Sprinkle each layer lightly with salt. Place the remainder of the sliced tomatoes over the top of the eggplants.

Cook as directed on page 78.

Variation:

Eggplants may also be stuffed as for Stuffed Zucchini in Tomato Sauce and Stuffed Zucchini in Yoghurt Sauce (see pages 79, 81).

Preparing stuffed vegetables for cooking. Note the special zucchini scoop in the centre of the picture.

EGGS

Eggs are plentiful in Lebanon and much use is made of them. They are prepared in a variety of ways — hard-boiled, fried, as omelettes, or in other dishes — and the flavour is generally enhanced by herbs, spices and flavourings.

Hard-boiled eggs have been relished from early times. They are often served with salad vegetables in an oil and lemon dressing, or on a platter with other foods for a light meal. A favourite recipe is *Luffet Byde*, in which the eggs are wrapped in a meat kafta mixture and simmered (see picture left, recipe page 85).

Omelettes of all types are extremely popular. They are usually cooked in olive oil rather than butter as in other cuisines. Often the mixture is spooned into the pan to make little omelettes or fried in a special pan which has round depressions in its surface for this purpose.

Egg dishes are eaten mainly for breakfast or lunch and are generally accompanied by Lebanese bread and salads.

Luffet Byde (page 85) with a selection of crisp salad vegetables.

Byde Mi'li
Fried Eggs in Olive Oil Ⓥ

Serves: 1
Cooking time: 5 minutes
2 eggs
olive oil
½ lemon
finely chopped fresh or dried mint or oregano

Fry the eggs in very hot olive oil, basting the yolks to give a white film.

Squeeze lemon juice over the top, garnish with mint or oregano and serve immediately, accompanied by Lebanese bread and whole spring onions.

To eat these eggs the Lebanese way, hold a fork in one hand and push bite-sized portions onto small pieces of Lebanese bread held in the other hand.

Parsley Omelettes
Ijjit b'Dounis Ⓥ

Makes: 20 small omelettes
Cooking time: approx 2 minutes per batch
4 eggs
1 cup chopped parsley or ½ cup mint and
  ½ cup parsley
1 teaspoon flour
salt and pepper
olive oil or substitute

Beat eggs and combine with dry ingredients. Spoon into hot oil to make small omelettes and cook. Repeat this procedure until all the mixture is used.

Brain Omelette
Ijjit N'kha

Serves: 2
Cooking time: 35 minutes
2 sets lamb's brains, steamed and sliced
salt and black pepper
3 eggs
2 spring onions, chopped finely
1 tablespoon olive oil or substitute

Sprinkle the sliced brains with salt and pepper.

Beat the eggs and season with salt and pepper. Mix in the spring onions.

Gently heat the oil in a frying pan and pour in the egg and onion mixture. Spread the sliced brains evenly over the top and cook over a very gentle heat until the eggs are just set — approx 20 minutes.

Place under a griller or slip the omelette onto a plate and return to the pan to cook the underside.

Eggplant Omelette
Ijjit Batinjaan Ⓥ

Serves: 4-6
Cooking time: 15-20 minutes
2 small or 1 large eggplant
1 onion, finely chopped
2 tablespoons olive oil or substitute
1-2 cloves garlic, crushed
6 eggs
salt and black pepper

Peel and cube the eggplant, and prepare for cooking as directed on page 20.

Fry the chopped onion in the oil until soft and golden. Add the crushed garlic, then the eggplant, and sauté until tender.

Beat the eggs, season with salt and pepper, and stir into the eggplant mixture. Cook over very low heat until the eggs are set.

Brown the top of the omelette under the griller or slip it onto a plate and return to the pan to cook the underside.

Eggs with Tomato
Byde b'Banadoura Ⓥ

Serves: 4-6
Cooking time: 20 minutes
4 ripe medium tomatoes
2 tablespoons water
4 eggs
salt and pepper
½ teaspoon ground cinnamon
¼ cup finely chopped parsley (optional)
¼ cup finely chopped spring onions (optional)
1 tablespoon olive oil or substitute

Wash, peel and quarter the tomatoes. Simmer them gently in the water in a covered pan until soft. Pour into a baking dish.

Beat eggs well and mix in salt, pepper, cinnamon, parsley and spring onions. Pour this mixture over the tomatoes.

Cook over a low heat, without stirring, until the eggs are set. Pour oil over the eggs and place under the griller to cook the top.

Zucchini and Egg Fritters

Ijjit Kousa Ⓥ

Makes: approx 12
Cooking time: 8-10 minutes per batch

1 clove garlic
1 teaspoon salt
4-6 spring onions
1 pinch pepper
¼ teaspoon mixed spices (see page 21)
1 cup zucchini pulp
5 eggs
¾ cup self-raising flour
½-1 cup finely chopped parsley
¼ cup chopped fresh mint or 1 teaspoon dried mint
olive or nut oil

Crush the garlic in a bowl with the salt. Mix in the spring onions, pepper and mixed spices. Add the mashed zucchini and the eggs. Beat well with a beater, then thoroughly mix in the flour. Add parsley and mint.

Spoon the mixture into a pan of hot oil and fry until the fritters are golden brown on both sides. Repeat this procedure until all the mixture is used.

Variation:
Add 1 tablespoon of olive or nut oil to the mixture. Pour it into a greased baking dish to a thickness of 2.5-4 cm (1-1½ in) and bake in a moderate oven until cooked — approx ¾ hour.

Luffet Byde

Egg Roll

Serves: 4-6
Cooking time: 30 minutes

2 cups Basic Kafta Mixture, omitting parsley
  (see page 65)
½ cup finely chopped parsley
3 hard-boiled eggs
½ cup ghee or substitute (see page 27)

With wet hands roll the kafta mixture into a ball and flatten it onto a wet board, forming a flat oblong shape, approximately 1.25 cm (½ in) in depth. Sprinkle the parsley over the top.

Shell the eggs and place end to end along the centre of mixture. Roll the mixture around the eggs to form a meat roll, join the ends together and smooth the meat all over with wet hands. Wind a long length of coarse white cotton thread around the roll in all directions to keep the meat together.

Heat the ghee in a saucepan, add the meat roll and cook until well browned all over. Cover, turn down the heat and simmer slowly until cooked through, turning the roll regularly and sprinkling a few drops of water over it occasionally to prevent it from drying out — approx 20-30 minutes. (Be careful not to overcook the meat.)

When cooked, remove the roll from the saucepan, cool, and remove the thread. Refrigerate before cutting in slices (see picture, page 82).

Serve with salads.

Tying cotton thread around Luffet Byde.

SALADS

Salads are an important part of the Lebanese menu. No meal is complete without a platter of crisp salad vegetables or a tossed salad.

The king of Lebanese salads is the famous *Tabbouleh*, made with parsley and bur'ghul. Another very popular salad is *Fattoush*, which includes chickweed and toasted cubes of bread and probably originated among the poorer people. Cooked salads and salads in which some of the ingredients are cooked and others raw are also well liked.

The ingredients for Lebanese salads must be as fresh as possible. They should be washed well and dried, and served cold and crisp. The traditional dressing is a simple combination of lemon juice and olive oil, with garlic, salt and black pepper.

The famous parsley salad, Tabbouleh (page 88).

Salad Dressing

Makes: 1 cup ⓥⓁ

½ cup lemon juice
½ cup olive oil
2 cloves garlic
1 teaspoon salt
¼ teaspoon black pepper

Mix the lemon juice and oil together. Crush the garlic to a paste with the salt and mix it into the oil and lemon juice. Add pepper.

Tabbouleh

Parsley Salad ⓥⓁ

Serves: 4

½ cup bur'ghul (see page 20)
8-10 spring onions
2 teaspoons salt
¼ teaspoon black pepper
¼ teaspoon mixed spices (see page 21)
5 cups very finely chopped parsley
¼ cup very finely chopped fresh mint or
　2 teaspoons dried mint
3 large tomatoes, finely chopped
approx ¼ cup lemon juice
¼ cup olive oil

Wash the bur'ghul and drain well by squeezing out excess water with cupped hands. Place in a bowl and refrigerate for at least 1 hour.

Trim the spring onions to leave about 20 cm (8 in) of green. Finely chop the white of the spring onions and mix it into the drained bur'ghul with the salt, pepper and spices. Finely chop the green of the spring onions and place it with parsley, mint and tomatoes on top of the bur'ghul mixture. Set aside in the refrigerator until ready to serve.

Just before serving, add the lemon juice and olive oil and toss well. Adjust salt and lemon juice to taste.

Tabbouleh is usually served in a wide based bowl or deep serving dish and garnished with lettuce leaves. When it is served as mezza a large spoonful is placed in a lettuce leaf, wrapped into a roll and eaten with the fingers.

Variation:
Add 1 small cucumber or ½ green pepper (both finely chopped) to the salad.

Fattoush

Peasant Salad ⓥⓁ

It is customary, although not essential, to include chickweed (baquli) in this salad. This weed is not sold commercially but grows wild in many gardens. It has soft green leaves and is considered very nourishing.

Serves: 6

1 cup very crisp toasted bread (preferably Lebanese),
　cubed and sprinkled with a little water
4 small cucumbers or 2 cups shredded lettuce or half
　of each
2 medium tomatoes
½-1 green pepper, chopped finely
½ cup finely chopped spring onions
½ cup finely chopped parsley
¼ cup finely chopped mint
1 cup finely chopped chickweed (optional)
½ cup Salad Dressing (see left)

Place all the ingredients in a bowl and toss well. Add the dressing and toss again. Adjust salt and lemon juice to taste.

Cabbage Salad
Salatit Malfouf ⓋⓁ

Serves: 6-8

1 small or ½ large green or red cabbage
½ teaspoon salt
½ cup Salad Dressing, omitting salt (see left)

Core the cabbage and remove any tough outer leaves.

Shred the cabbage leaves finely and sprinkle with salt. Rub the salt well into the leaves.

Place the salted leaves in a colander, cover with a weighted plate to extract excess moisture and set aside for half an hour.

When the cabbage leaves are soft, squeeze them tightly to remove excess moisture and place them in a salad bowl. Pour the dressing over the top and toss well. Adjust salt and lemon juice to taste.

Endive Salad
Hindbeh m'Tabbal ⓋⓁ

Serves: 6
Cooking time: ½-1 hour

1 large bunch of endives (approx size of a
    large lettuce)
1 large onion, chopped finely
1 teaspoon salt
¼ teaspoon pepper
¼ cup lemon juice
¼ cup olive oil

Wash and chop the endive leaves, then boil in a large pot of boiling water until tender — approx ½-1 hour. Lightly drain and place in a bowl. Add the chopped raw onion, salt, pepper, lemon juice and olive oil. Toss, cool and refrigerate before serving.

Cooked Vegetable Salad
Salatit Khoodra ⓋⓁ

Serves: 4

4 cups sliced zucchini, string beans, chokos or
    cauliflower pieces, or a combination of 2 or more
¾ cup Salad Dressing (see left)

Partially cook the vegetables in boiling water. Drain and cool. Add dressing and toss well. Adjust salt and lemon juice to taste.

Cauliflower with Avocado and Tahini Sauce
Ar'nabit b'Abocarto Taratoor ⓋⓁ

Serves: 4
Cooking time: 20 minutes

1 small or ½ large cauliflower
boiling water
2 teaspoons salt
2 cups Avocado with Tahini Sauce (see page 26)

Place cauliflower in a saucepan with enough boiling water to cover. Add salt and cook until just tender. Remove, drain.

Pour the sauce over the cauliflower.

Serve hot or cold.

Spinach Stalks
Dlough Silih ⓋⓁ

This recipe requires only the spinach stalks. Use the leaves for Stuffed Spinach Leaves (page 79), Spinach Soup (page 42) or Spinach Stew (page 70).

Makes: approx 4 cups
Cooking time: ½ hour

500 g (1 lb) spinach stalks (without leaves)
boiling water
2 teaspoons salt
pinch of baking powder
1 cup Tahini Sauce (see page 26)

Chop the spinach stalks into 5 cm (2 in) strips. Place in boiling water with salt and baking powder and simmer until soft and tender — approx 50 minutes.

Drain stalks and mash or leave sliced. Gently mix in the Tahini Sauce.

Serve cold.

PICKLES

Before refrigeration and easy transport, the preservation of food was a great problem in the hot countries of the Middle East, particularly in isolated areas. Pickling was originally devised to overcome this problem, however the result was so delicious that pickles are still an important part of the diet.

Almost every Lebanese household has a selection of home-made pickles. They are an important part of the mezza and are often served as accompaniments for the main course.

The pickling solution we have given uses equal quantities of brine and vinegar, however some people prefer to use all brine or all vinegar or other proportions of the two. Always mix the solution in clean, grease-free glass, porcelain or enamel containers.

For successful pickling you must use prime, fresh vegetables which have been thoroughly washed and dried. Cucumbers and eggplants should be tiny — no more than 10cm x 2.5cm (4in x 1in) — and can be ordered from your local market or greengrocer.

Store the pickles in sterilized glass or porcelain jars with airtight lids. Ensure that the solution completely covers the vegetables and that there are no air bubbles in the jar. They will keep for about two months.

Pickled Cucumber (page 92), Pickled Cauliflower (page 93) and Pickled Turnips (page 93).

Pickling Solution ⓥⓛ

Makes: 5 cups
Cooking time: 10 minutes

½ cup cooking salt
2 cups water
2½ cups vinegar

Stir the salt into the water. Bring to the boil and boil for 3 minutes. Add the vinegar.

Pickled Cucumber

Kabees Kh'yaar ⓥⓛ

Cooking time: 10 minutes

1.25 kg (2½ lb) very small thin cucumbers
1 hot pepper
5 cups Pickling Solution (see above)
1 tablespoon olive oil

Wash and dry the cucumbers and place them in a large sterilized jar with the hot pepper. Cover with the pickling solution and add the olive oil. Seal with an airtight lid and set aside for at least 7 days before eating.

Pickled Eggplant

Kabees Batinjaan ⓥⓛ

Cooking time: 40 minutes

1 kg (2 lb) very small thin eggplants (see page 91)
4 cloves garlic
1 teaspoon salt
2 hot peppers
5 cups Pickling Solution (see left)
1 tablespoon olive oil

Wash the eggplants and discard stems.

Place the eggplants in a pot of boiling water and bring back to the boil. Cover and simmer for 3 minutes. Remove from the water and leave to drain for approx half an hour.

Crush the garlic and salt to a paste. Chop up one of the hot peppers and mix it into the garlic.

Make a deep lengthwise slit in each side of each eggplant. Dab a pinch of the garlic and hot pepper mixture into the slits.

Place the eggplants and the remaining hot pepper in a sterilized large glass jar. Cover with the pickling solution and add olive oil. Seal with an airtight lid and set aside for at least 2 weeks before eating.

Variation:
Chopped walnuts can be added to the garlic and pepper mixture.

Pickled Onions

Kabees Bassal ⓥⓛ

1.25 kg (2½ lb) small firm white onions
1 hot pepper
5 cups Pickling Solution (see left)

Peel the onions and place in a sterilized glass jar with the hot pepper. Cover with pickling solution, seal with an airtight lid and set aside for at least 7-10 days before eating.

Pickled Turnips

Kabees Lifit Ⓥ Ⓛ

Cooking time: 10 minutes

1 kg (2 lb) turnips
2 large beetroot (for colour)
1 hot pepper
5 cups **Pickling Solution** (see left)

Peel the turnips and beetroot, wash very well and slice into quarters. Place in a sterilized glass jar with the hot pepper. Cover with pickling solution, seal with an airtight lid and set aside for at least 10 days before eating.

Pickled Cauliflower

Kabees Ar'nabit Ⓥ Ⓛ

Cooking time: 20 minutes

1 medium cauliflower
1 large beetroot (for colour)
5 cups **Pickling Solution** (see left)

Break or cut the cauliflower into flowerettes and wash. Place in a pot of water, bring to the boil and simmer for 3 minutes. Drain well and place in sterilized pickling jars.

Wash and peel the beetroot, cut into quarters and add to the cauliflower.

Cover with pickling solution, seal with an airtight lid and set aside for at least 3 days before eating.

Pickled Green Olives

Zaitoon Ukhdor Ⓥ Ⓛ

2 kg (4 lb) raw green olives
coarse salt
water
few lemon wedges
1 hot green pepper (optional)

Wash the olives well in lukewarm water. Split each olive two or three times with a sharp fine knife or leave intact. Place in a sterilized glass or earthenware container and cover with salted water, using ½ cup salt to every 2.5 litres (4 pints) of water. Place a small plate on top to prevent olives floating on top of the solution. Cover and leave to soak for 6-8 weeks, changing the salted water every week.

Make a brine by boiling together 1 cup salt to every 4 cups of water. Allow to cool.

Drain the soaked olives and place in a sterilized glass or earthenware container with the lemon wedges and hot green pepper. Cover with the cool brine, replace the plate and seal with an airtight lid. Set aside for approx 6-8 weeks until the bitter taste disappears.

Pickled Black Olives

Zaitoon Uswid Ⓥ Ⓛ

2 kg (4 lb) raw black olives
1 cup coarse salt
½ cup olive oil
½ cup brown vinegar (optional)

Wash the olives well in lukewarm water. Place in a sterilized glass or earthenware container and cover with water. Place a small plate on top to prevent olives floating on top of the water. Cover and leave to soak for 6 days, changing the water every day.

Drain the soaked olives and place in a sterilized glass or earthenware container. Add the salt, olive oil and vinegar and mix well. Seal with an airtight lid and set aside for approx 2-4 weeks until the bitter taste disappears.

SWEETS

Lebanese cakes, pastries, desserts, jams and preserves are very sweet. They are always served to visitors with coffee, and are often eaten as snacks between meals. However they are not necessarily served as desserts at the end of a meal, but may be replaced by a bowl of fresh fruit in season.

The most popular Lebanese sweets are *B'learwa* and *K'naafeh* pastries which, like many recipes, are saturated in a fragrant sugar syrup. They are made commercially, but like most foods they are even more delicious when fresh from the home kitchen.

Some Lebanese sweets are traditionally made to celebrate religious or family festivities. *Oo'whamat*, for example, are made for the *Gh'taas* (baptism of Christ) celebration, *Ma'amool b'Jowz* are special Easter cakes, and *Meghli* is a rice pudding served to well-wishers when a baby is born.

Although many of these sweets appear very intricate, most of them are surprisingly easy to make and with a little practice you can become a real expert.

The traditional Easter walnut cakes, Ma'amool b'Jowz (page 102).

Plain Rice Pudding
Ruz b'Haleeb Ⓥ

Serves: 6
Cooking time: 45 minutes

3½ cups milk
½ cup sugar
½ cup rice, washed and drained
½ cup water
1 teaspoon rosewater or orange blossom water
   (see page 21)
½ cup blanched slivered almonds for decoration

Bring the milk and sugar to the boil. Add the rice, mixed with the water, and stir until it comes to the boil again. Turn down the heat to a low simmer and cook gently until the mixture becomes very creamy — approx 45 minutes. (Add a little more milk during cooking if necessary.)

Add the rosewater or orange blossom water, stirring until bubbles appear on the surface. Remove from the heat and cool slightly, then pour into a bowl and refrigerate.

Serve chilled, decorated with slivered almonds.

Ground Rice Pudding
M'hal'labeeyeh Ⓥ

Serves: 6-8
Cooking time: 20 minutes

2 tablespoons cornflour/cornstarch
¼ cup ground rice
1.25 litres (2 pints) milk
1 cup sugar
1 teaspoon rosewater or orange blossom water
   (see page 21)
¼ cup blanched slivered almonds or some
   Crystallized Flowers for decoration (see
   page 105)

Mix the cornflour/cornstarch and ground rice to a paste with a little of the milk.

Mix the remaining milk with the sugar and bring to the boil. Warm the paste with a few tablespoons of the boiling milk.

Lower the heat to a simmer and, using a wooden spoon, gradually stir the warm paste into the milk. (Be careful not to scrape the bottom of the pot with the spoon so that you do not dislodge particles of burned milk which may have occurred during boiling.)

Continue stirring the mixture until it thickens enough to coat the spoon. Stir for a further minute, then remove from the heat and stir in the rosewater or orange blossom water. Cool slightly, pour into individual dishes and refrigerate.

Serve chilled, decorated with slivered almonds or Crystallized Flowers.

Meghli
Festive Rice Pudding Ⓥ

Serves: 8
Cooking time: 1¼ hours

1 cup ground rice
5 cups cold water
1 cup sugar
1 teaspoon aniseed or ½ teaspoon powdered
1 teaspoon fennel seeds or ½ teaspoon powdered
1 teaspoon caraway seeds or ½ teaspoon powdered
2 teaspoons ground cinnamon
½ cup blanched slivered almonds for decoration

Mix the ground rice to a smooth paste with some of the cold water. Add the sugar, aniseed, fennel, caraway and cinnamon.

Bring the remaining water to the boil. Add the ground rice mixture gradually, stirring vigorously with a wooden spoon. Continue stirring until it comes to the boil again, then lower the heat and simmer, stirring occasionally, until cooked — approx 1 hour.

The mixture is cooked when it is thick enough to coat the spoon. Cool it slightly, pour into individual bowls and refrigerate.

Serve chilled, decorated with the almonds.

Atter
Sugar Syrup Ⓥ

This syrup will keep well if stored in an airtight jar. When used for sweetening pastries it should be cold and poured over very hot pastry, otherwise it will not penetrate the pastry.

Makes: 3 cups
Cooking time: 10 minutes

3 cups sugar
1½ cups water
1 tablespoon lemon juice
1 teaspoon rosewater or orange blossom water
   (see page 21)

Dissolve sugar in water, add lemon juice and bring to the boil. Skim the foam from the surface and continue to boil, stirring occasionally until syrup thickens slightly — approx 10 minutes. Add the rosewater or orange blossom water towards the end of the cooking time.

Stand syrup to cool.

Variations:
• A thicker syrup can be made by further vigorous boiling.
• For a thinner syrup, add more water and re-boil a little longer.

Syrup Cheese
Helwhaat El Jibni Ⓥ

This recipe may be intricate and difficult to master at first but the result is worthwhile. When well made the taste and texture of this sweet is extremely unique and to eat it is a delightful experience. (Lebanese cheese is mature enough for cooking when a small piece melted over an open flame can be pulled into a thread — approx 4-6 days old.)

Serves: 4-6
Cooking time: approx 30 minutes

500 g unsalted mature white Lebanese cheese or unsalted Mozzarella cheese
1½ cups boiling water
1½ cups semolina
2 cups hot Atter syrup (see left)

Slice the cheese.

Place the water in a saucepan and bring it to the boil. Gently stir in the sliced cheese until it melts (only a few seconds), then drain off all but 1 or 2 tablespoons of the water.

Return the cheese to the heat and stir with a wooden spoon, gradually adding the semolina, then gradually stir in ¼ cup of hot syrup on a low heat for about 3 minutes making sure that you stir it vigorously to avoid sticking.

Lightly moisten a baking tray with about 2 tablespoons of the hot syrup. Remove the hot cheese mixture (it will resemble dough) from the stove and quickly pour it onto the moistened tray. Wearing rubber gloves to protect the hands from the heat, quickly flatten the cheese dough into a paper thin sheet over the bottom of the tray.

Sprinkle a little more syrup over the dough in the baking tray, fold the edges of the sheet into the centre and then again until it becomes a square lump. Flatten out the lump back into a thin sheet, moistening with more syrup if necessary. The dough should now resemble a piece of fine cloth. Tear the "cloth" into strips and drop them into the remainder of the warm syrup.

Serve cool or chilled, plain or with Ushta (see page 27).

Oo'whamat
Dough Balls in Syrup Ⓥ

Makes: approx 50 balls
Cooking time: 5 minutes per batch

3½ cups plain flour
7.5 g (¼ oz) dried yeast or 15 g (½ oz) fresh yeast
2½ cups lukewarm water
1 teaspoon sugar
4 cups Atter syrup (see left)
nut or corn oil for frying
ground cinnamon (optional)

Warm a mixing bowl and sift the flour into it.

Dissolve the yeast in ¼ cup of the lukewarm water, add the sugar and set aside until it rises and foams.

Beat the remaining water into the yeast, then gradually add the flour, beating constantly until the mixture becomes a sticky batter. Cover with a damp cloth and place in a warm spot to rise — approx 1¼ hours. During the first hour beat the mixture vigorously at quarter hour intervals.

Place 5 cm (2 in) oil in a frying pan and heat until very hot. With a wet teaspoon scoop up the dough and drop it into the hot oil. The dough balls will swell up and float to the top, at which stage you should turn the heat down to medium and keep cooking until they are crisp and golden brown.

Remove the dough balls from the oil, drain on absorbent paper, and while still hot immerse briefly in cool Atter syrup. Set aside and sprinkle with cinnamon.

Serve hot or cold.

K'naafeh

String Pastry Sweets Ⓥ

Serves: 8
Cooking time: 55 minutes

185 g (6½ oz) k'naafeh pastry, commercial or home
made (see below)
½ cup ghee (see page 27) or unsalted butter, melted
2 cups cold rosewater or orange blossom water
(see page 21)
Vanilla cream filling:
¾ cup cornflour/cornstarch
750 ml (1½ pints) milk
150 ml (¼ pint) cream
2 teaspoons vanilla essence

Place the k'naafeh pastry in a large bowl and separate the "strings" as much as possible. Pour in the melted ghee or butter and work it in with the fingers, making sure that each pastry string is thoroughly greased. (Traditionally the string is now put through a grinder and crumbled, however it is just as delicious when left whole.)

Vanilla cream filling:
Make a paste with the cornflour/cornstarch and some of the milk, and set aside.

Heat the milk and cream together in a saucepan. Remove from the heat and mix a little of the hot milk and cream into the cornflour/cornstarch paste to warm, then pour the paste into the hot milk mixture, stirring constantly. Return to the heat and simmer until thick, stirring constantly to avoid lumps. (If it does get lumpy, use an eggbeater.)

Mix in the vanilla essence.

To assemble the k'naafeh:
Place half the pastry strings evenly over the bottom of a 25 cm (10 in) baking dish and cover with the filling, then place the remainder of the pastry in an even layer on top and press down firmly.

Bake in a preheated oven at 180°C (350°F) for 45 minutes, then turn up to 230°C (450°F) and bake for a further 10-15 minutes or until it is a light golden colour on top.

Remove the K'naafeh from the oven and while still hot pour the cool rosewater or orange blossom water over it. Serve hot or cold.

Variation:
Crumbled unsalted Lebanese white cheese, Mozzarella or Ricotta can be substituted for the vanilla cream filling.

K'naafeh Pastry

Pre-prepared k'naafeh pastry can be purchased from Lebanese bakeries and delicatessens, and from some continental delicatessens. The recipe is extremely intricate and is not usually made in the home. It is included here, for the keen and the curious.

The pastry should resemble white vermicelli. To make it you will need a k'naafeh strainer, which is a metal container with a line of holes in the bottom to allow the batter to pour through in fine threads.

1 kg (2 lb) plain flour
2 cups water
1¼ cups milk

Mix all the ingredients together and knead into a smooth dough. Gradually add enough water to form a thin batter.

Heat a heavy griddle over a low heat and pour the batter onto it, passing it first through a k'naafeh strainer. The batter will come through the strainer in long string-like strips and solidify on the hot griddle.

As soon as the k'naafeh strips are set, remove and set aside, and continue making more strips until all the batter is used.

Boorrma

String Pastry Rolls Ⓥ

Makes: 15 rolls

200 g (6½ oz) k'naafeh pastry, commercial or
home made (see K'naafeh recipe, this page)
125 g (¼ lb) ghee (see page 27) or unsalted
butter, melted
1 cup walnut pieces or a mixture of walnuts,
almonds and pistachio nuts, finely chopped
or coarsely ground
1½ tablespoons sugar
1½ cups cold Atter syrup (see page 96)

Prepare the k'naafeh pastry for cooking by greasing well with the melted ghee or butter as in the recipe for K'naafeh, but leave the strings whole.

Mix the chopped nuts with the sugar.

Divide the k'naafeh pastry into strands about 20 cm (8 in) long and 6.5 cm (2½ in) wide. Place one tablespoon of the nut and sugar mixture at the top of one strand. Put the round handle of a wooden spoon over the mixture and roll the pastry around it to form a roll. Remove the spoon handle. Continue this process until all the rolls are made.

Place the rolls on a baking tray and bake in a moderate oven until golden — approx 20-25 minutes. Remove the rolls from the oven and while still hot pour the Atter syrup over them.

Variation:
Make the rolls longer and thicker. When cooked pour cool Atter syrup over them, then slice into 2.5 cm (1 in) rounds.

A platter of B'learwa (page 100) and Boorma (page 98), Syrup Cheese (page 97) with Ushta (page 27) and Lebanese Coffee (page 107).

B'learwa

Sweet Layered Pastries Ⓥ

If filo pastry is exposed to air it will become dry. Before commencing this recipe, lay all the pastry flat on a tray and cover with greaseproof paper then a damp cloth and remove only one sheet at a time.

Makes: 28 pieces
Cooking time: 35 minutes

250 g (½ lb) melted butter, preferably unsalted
500 g (1 lb) filo pastry
2 cups walnut pieces or a mixture of walnuts, almonds and pistachio nuts, finely chopped or coarsely ground
3 tablespoons sugar
1½ cups cold Atter syrup (see page 96)

Using a pastry brush, paint the sides and bottom of a round or square baking dish, approx 30cm x 45cm (12in x 18in), with butter.

Paint one of the pastry sheets with butter and place it in the baking tray, then paint a second sheet and place it on top of the first, overlapping or folding in the sides of the sheet if necessary. Continue in this way until half the amount of sheets have been buttered (six or more layers).

Mix the chopped nuts with the sugar and spread evenly over the top sheet of pastry in the tray. Cover with the remaining pastry sheets, buttering them as for the lower layers. Be sure to brush the top of the final sheet with butter.

Cut deep diagonal lines down and across the surface of the pastry to form diamond-shaped slices.

Bake on the centre shelf of a pre-heated oven at 160-180°C (325-350°F) for 30 minutes, then turn the temperature up to 230-240°C (450-475°F) and bake for a further 5-10 minutes, or until the pastry puffs and is a light golden colour. Remove from the oven and while still hot pour the cold Atter syrup over it.

Variation:
Butter and stack the layers of pastry as above until the stack is 7 mm (¼ in) thick. Cut the stack into 7.5 cm (3 in) squares. Draw up the edges of each square and pinch the corners to form tart shells. Fill each shell with the nut and sugar mixture.

Atayif

Lebanese Pancakes Ⓥ

Serves: 8
Cooking time: approx 8 minutes each

Batter:
45 g (1½ oz) fresh yeast or 7.5 g (¼ oz) dried yeast
1 teaspoon sugar
1¼ cups lukewarm water
1½ cups plain flour

Topping:
3 cups cold Atter syrup (see page 96)

Dissolve the yeast and sugar together in ½ cup of the lukewarm water. Stand in a warm place until it begins to bubble — approx 10 minutes.

Sift the flour into a warm bowl and make a well in the centre, then pour in the yeast mixture and rub it into the flour.

Pour the remainder of the lukewarm water into the flour and stir until it is a smooth batter. Cover with a cloth and stand in a warm place for 1 hour or until the batter rises and is bubbly.

Thoroughly grease the inside of a heavy frying pan by rubbing it with a paper towel dipped in oil, then heat until very hot. Turn down the heat to medium and drop 1 tablespoon of batter into the pan. Gently tilt the pan from side to side to help the batter spread evenly, but make sure it remains round and thick. When the pancake begins to bubble and comes away easily from the pan, flip it over and cook the other side. Repeat this process until all the batter is used.

As the pancakes are cooked, pile them on a plate, one on top of the other. While still hot dip each one into cold Atter syrup and serve, either by themselves or accompanied by Ushta (see page 27) or whipped cream sprinkled with chopped nuts.

Atayif Mihshi

Stuffed Lebanese Pancakes Ⓥ

Serves: 8
Cooking time: approx 10 minutes

1 quantity Atayif batter (see left)
2 cups finely chopped walnuts mixed with 3
    tablespoons sugar and 2 teaspoons ground
    cinnamon
3 cups cold Atter syrup (see page 96)
olive or nut oil for frying

Make pancakes from batter as in previous recipe, but cook one side only. Set aside, one on top of the other, until all are cooked.

Cover the uncooked side of each pancake with the walnut and sugar mixture. Fold into half circles and pinch the edges to secure.

Deep fry the stuffed pancakes in hot oil until a golden colour — approx 2-3 minutes. Drain well on absorbent paper and while still hot dip in the cold Atter syrup.

Serve hot or cold.

Variations:
Substitute one of the following fillings for the walnut mixture:
• 2 cups Ushta (see page 27)
• 500 g (1 lb) unsalted Lebanese white cheese, grated
• 500 g (1 lb) Ricotta cheese

Orange and Coconut Cake

Kark El Laemoon Jose El Hind Ⓥ

Cooking time: 45 minutes

250 g (½ lb) butter
¼ cup sugar
4 eggs
¼ teaspoon baking powder
1 cup self-raising flour
1 cup semolina
1½ cups desiccated coconut
1½ teaspoons ground cinnamon
1 tablespoon grated orange peel
½ cup walnut pieces
½ cup orange juice
¼ cup sweet wine or sherry (optional)
½ cup blanched slivered almonds
3 cups cold Atter syrup (see page 96)

Cream the butter and sugar, and gradually beat in the eggs.

Sift the baking powder with the flour and mix in the semolina, 1 cup of the desiccated coconut, the cinnamon, orange peel and walnuts.

With a wooden spoon lightly stir the dry ingredients into the creamed butter, adding orange juice and wine or sherry. Pour into a well greased and lightly floured baking dish, approx 23 cm (9 in). Decorate with slivered almonds and bake at 180°C (350°F) for 45 minutes.

When the cake is cooked and golden brown on top, remove it from the oven and while still hot spoon the Atter syrup over the top. Sprinkle with the remaining ½ cup of desiccated coconut.

Ma'amool b'Jowz

Easter Walnut Cakes ⓥ

Makes: 12-15 small cakes
Cooking time: 20 minutes

Pastry:
750 g (1½ lb) semolina
1 cup sugar
500 g (1 lb) butter
boiling water
Filling:
500 g (1 lb) fresh walnut pieces
½ cup sugar
½ teaspoon rosewater (see page 21)
¼ cup cold water
Topping:
2 cups icing sugar

Pastry:
Place the semolina and sugar in a large bowl and mix together thoroughly.

Melt the butter and bring it to the boil, then gradually blend it into the semolina and sugar mixture. Knead well, then set aside in an airtight container for at least one hour or up to 24 hours.

Knead the mixture again, pouring in enough boiling water to make a soft pliable dough. (It is a good idea to wear rubber gloves to protect your hands from the heat.)

Filling:
Crush the walnuts into very small pieces and mix in the sugar.

Add the rosewater to the cold water and mix into the walnut and sugar mixture.

To assemble:
Mould the pastry into small balls about 5 cm (2 in) in diameter. Hollow out the centre of each ball with your index finger by pressing around the inside of the ball to make a shell about 7 mm (¼ in) thick.

Fill the hollow shell with the filling mixture and close the top of the shell by pressing the dough together.

Flatten the shell into a pie shape by pressing lightly between the palms of the hands. Make a design on top with the side and prongs of a fork. (A special mould called a *taabeh* can be used if you prefer.)

Place the cakes on a baking tray and cook in a very hot oven, 230°C (450°F), until lightly browned — approx 20 minutes.

Topping:
Sprinkle sifted icing sugar generously over the top of the cakes.

Store in airtight containers.

Variations:
• The following pastry may be substituted for the semolina pastry:

3½ cups plain flour
250 g (½ lb) unsalted butter or ghee (see page 27)
1 tablespoon rosewater or orange blossom water (see page 27)
4 tablespoons milk

Sift the flour and work in the butter by hand. Add the rosewater or orange blossom water and knead until the pastry is soft and easy to shape. Make as before but bake in a preheated slow oven, 180°C (350°F), for 20-25 minutes. (When cooked, the pastry will still be soft, but it will harden when cool. Do not allow it to brown as the taste will not be as good.)

• The following filling may be substituted for the walnut filling:

1 kg (2 lb) dates
125 g (¼ lb) butter

Crush the dates and mix into the batter. Knead together until they are well blended.

Semolina and Yoghurt Slices

Mummoora ⓥ

Makes: 15 slices
Cooking time: approx 50 minutes

2½ cups semolina
2 cups yoghurt
½ cup sugar
125 g (¼ lb) butter, melted
1 teaspoon baking powder
2 cups cool Atter syrup (see page 96)

Mix together the semolina, yoghurt, sugar, butter and baking powder. Spread the mixture evenly in a well greased 25 cm (10 in) baking tray and bake in a 180°C (350°F) oven until cooked through and lightly brown on top — approx 50 minutes.

Remove from the oven and while still hot cut diagonal lines through the cooked mixture to make diamond-shaped slices, then pour the cool Atter syrup over the top.

Serve hot or cold, either by itself or with Ushta (see page 27) or whipped cream.

Variation:
Substitute ½ cup desiccated coconut for ½ cup of the semolina.

Delicious syrupy Oo'whamat (page 97), with Lebanese coffee cups, a Middle Eastern coffee pot and a Lebanese rakweh (far right).

Shortbread Biscuits

Gh'raybeh Ⓥ

Makes: 30 biscuits
Cooking time: 25 minutes

500 g (1 lb) butter, preferably unsalted
1 cup caster sugar
7-8 cups plain flour, sifted
¼ cup blanched almonds for decoration

Cream the butter until it is white. Gradually beat in the sugar and continue beating for a further 5 minutes or until the mixture is smooth and creamy. Mix in the flour and knead by hand. The dough should be very soft, but if it is too soft for moulding, knead in a little more flour.

Mould the dough into small balls about the size of large walnuts. Press each ball down to make a flat bottom and place a blanched almond on top.

Place the biscuits on a baking tray (not too close together) and bake in a 150-160°C (300-325°F) oven for 20-30 minutes. Be careful not to overcook or brown them — they should still be white when they come out of the oven or the taste will deteriorate.

Variation:

When you have moulded the small balls, roll them into long sausage shapes, approx 10cm x 1.25cm (4in x ½in). Join the ends to form small circles and decorate by sprinkling chopped blanched almonds on top. Cook as above.

Sesame Seed Biscuits

Biscorti El Soom Soom Ⓥ

Makes: approx 45 biscuits
Cooking time: 20-25 minutes

250 g (½ lb) butter or margarine
¾ cup sugar
3 teaspoons vanilla essence
1 egg
⅓ cup milk
4½ cups self-raising flour
1 beaten egg yolk or 2 tablespoons milk for glazing
¼ cup sesame seeds

Cream together the butter, sugar and vanilla until smooth. Beat in the egg thoroughly, then add the milk. Stir in the flour and knead for a few seconds.

Taking walnut size pieces of dough, roll into long narrow strips, 10 cm (4 in) long and 1.25 cm (½ in) wide. Twist each strip into a circle, coil or any other shape. Brush lightly with the beaten egg yolk or milk and sprinkle with sesame seeds.

Place the biscuits on a well greased baking tray and bake in a moderate oven, 180°C (350°F), until golden — approx 20-25 minutes.

Orange Peel in Syrup

Mrubba Ziffair Ⓥ

The orange peel for this recipe may be collected over a period and kept fresh by storing in the refrigerator in an airtight container.

6 large or 8 small thin-skinned oranges for peel
2 cups sugar
2 cups water
1 tablespoon lemon juice

Scrape the surface of the oranges with a fork, then peel from the top to bottom with a sharp knife to make six segment strips. Scrape off some of the excess pith from the peel, then boil the peel until soft — approx 30 minutes. Drain well and soak in cold water for 24 hours, changing the water several times.

Roll up each strip and with a large needle, thread onto a heavy cotton thread, making a "necklace", to prevent the rolls from unravelling.

Bring the sugar and water to the boil, add the lemon juice and continue to boil for a further 5 minutes. Drop the "necklace" into the boiling syrup, turn down the heat and simmer slowly, stirring occasionally with a wooden spoon, until the syrup thickens enough to thickly coat the back of the spoon.

Lift the necklace out of the syrup, remove the thread and drop the rolls into a jar. Allow the syrup to cool slightly, then pour over the rolls, making sure they are all covered. Seal with an airtight lid.

Serve rolls either with the syrup or rolled in sugar as crystallized fruit.

Fig Jam
Mrubba Teen Ⓥ

If you cannot buy pre-roasted sesame seeds, you can roast your own by placing them on a hot heavy-based frying pan and stirring until slightly browned.

Makes: 1.75 kg (3½ lb)
Cooking time: 50 minutes

1 kg (2 lb) fresh figs
750 g (1½ lb) sugar
1½ cups boiling water
1 tablespoon lemon juice
¾ cup walnut pieces (optional)
1 tablespoon roasted sesame seeds
2 teaspoons ground aniseed (optional)
¼ teaspoon powdered gum arabic (optional)

Wash the figs, then chop them up and place in a large mixing bowl. Add the sugar, mix well and allow to stand for 3 hours or more.

Place the fig and sugar mixture in a large saucepan and simmer until juice appears — approx 5 minutes. Turn heat to high and boil for 3 minutes. Add boiling water and lemon juice and boil steadily until the figs become very soft and tender and the water is absorbed — approx 35 minutes. Add walnut pieces, sesame seeds, aniseed and cook and stir for a further 5 minutes.

Remove from the heat and mix in the gum arabic powder. Cool slightly and pour into jars. Seal with airtight lids.

Variation:
Dried figs can be used instead of fresh figs, but they must be soaked overnight in enough water to *just* cover them — do not drain.

Pumpkin Jam
Tutlit ya'Teen Ⓥ

Cooking time: 35 minutes

1 pumpkin
sugar
water
1 tablespoon lemon juice
¼ teaspoon powdered gum arabic (optional)
½ cup blanched almonds, slivered

Peel and seed the pumpkin, then grate or grind the flesh and measure by cups.

Measure 1 cup of sugar and ½ cup of water for every cup of pumpkin flesh.

Place the sugar and water in a saucepan and stir over a low heat until dissolved. Bring to the boil, add lemon juice, turn down the heat to a simmer and stir constantly with a wooden spoon until the syrup is thick enough to thickly coat the back of the spoon.

Stir in the grated pumpkin flesh and, still stirring, continue to simmer until the mixture becomes soft and transparent. Add the gum arabic powder and cook for a further 3 minutes.

Remove from the heat and stir in the slivered almonds. Allow to cool slightly, then pour into jars. Seal with airtight lids.

Crystallized Flowers
Zah'rit Succar Ⓥ

egg white
fruit blossom, violets, rose petals or mint leaves
caster sugar

Beat the egg white with a fork and pour it over the blossom, petals or leaves. Dip them into the caster sugar, then set aside on crinkled kitchen paper to dry in a cool place.

Use for decorating puddings, cakes and other sweets.

Tahini b'Asel
Tahini and Honey Spread Ⓥ

Mix 2 parts tahini (see page 21) with one part honey for a sweet, nourishing spread.

BEVERAGES

In Lebanon the most popular drink is iced water! Other important non-alcoholic drinks are coffee, tea and sweet cordials, while favourite alcoholic beverages are arack, beer and wine.

A jug of iced water is always set on the table for each meal. At other times water is often drunk from a *breah*, which is a special water ewer with a spout. The breah is held above head level and water is poured directly into the mouth without the mouth touching the spout. It takes practice to master this method of drinking, but it is hygienic and certainly saves washing tumblers!

Coffee drinking is a ritual in Lebanon and a visitor is always offered a cup as soon as he enters the house. Sugar is added to the coffee before it is brewed, so the guest is asked whether he likes it sweet, medium or without sugar. The coffee is served in very small cups, sometimes smaller than demitasse and often without handles. It is poured in the kitchen and presented on a tray, and the cups are handed around to each person.

If a guest does not want coffee he is offered tea or a cold cordial. Tea is always served weak and generally with slices of lemon. The traditional cordials are made from a thick fruit or fragrant syrup and diluted with water.

Alcoholic beverages are served with the mezza. The most popular of these is arack, a colourless but very potent anisated liquid which turns white as soon as water is added. Beers and wines of all types are imported into the country, but there are also many good local ones.

Lebanese Coffee
Ahweh Ⓥ

Lebanese coffee is traditionally made in a rakweh, which is a small copper or aluminium pot with a long handle (see picture, page 103), however a small saucepan with a pouring lip is a suitable substitute. Many people insist on roasting and grinding the beans just before making the coffee. If you do not want to do this, use the powdered Turkish coffee available at delicatessens and specialist food stores. Ordinary instant coffee is unsuitable.

For each demitasse cup of coffee, you will need:
1 demitasse cup of water
1-1½ level teaspoons sugar
1 heaped teaspoon powdered coffee (not instant)

Measure the water into a rakweh or small saucepan. Add the sugar and dissolve it by bringing the water to the boil and stirring. Remove from the heat, stir in the coffee, and very slowly bring to the boil again.

As soon as the coffee begins to rise, take it off the heat and allow to recede, then place it back on the heat to rise again. Repeat this procedure three times to extract maximum flavour from the coffee without overboiling it. Good Lebanese Coffee will have a thick sediment in the bottom and a brown froth on top. This froth is called "ushta" (not to be confused with milk cream which is also called ushta).

Serve the coffee by pouring a little at a time into each cup so that the coffee, sediment and "ushta" are evenly distributed.

Alternative method: Mix the coffee and sugar to a paste with a little of the water. Heat until it begins to bubble, add remainder of water and proceed as above.

Red Rosewater Cordial
Sharaab Elwarid Ⓥ

Makes: 4 cups syrup
Cooking time: 15 minutes
few drops of red food colouring
4 cups Atter syrup (see page 96)
iced water

Mix the food colouring with the Atter syrup, pour into a bottle with an airtight lid and store in the refrigerator. Dilute 2 tablespoons of syrup in a glass of iced water and serve as a cold cordial drink.

Mulberry Syrup
Sharaab Ettoot Ⓥ

Cooking time: 20 minutes
mulberries
sugar

Place fresh, fully ripe black mulberries, together with a few red ones, in a muslin bag. Wearing rubber gloves, press the juice from the mulberries through the bag and into an earthenware or enamel container.

Measure the juice into an enamel or ceramic cooking pot and add 2 cups of sugar for every cup of juice.

Boil the mixture vigorously, stirring with a wooden spoon until the syrup thickens. Remove from the heat, cool until tepid and pour into bottles.

Leave until completely cool, then seal with airtight lids and store. When a bottle is unsealed for use, it should be kept in the refrigerator.

Use as a syrup on sweets or dilute 2 tablespoons in a glass of iced water to make a cordial drink.

Tamarind Syrup
Sharaab El Tamarin Ⓥ

Tamarind pods can be purchased at Lebanese or Indian shops and some continental delicatessens.

Makes: 3 cups syrup
Cooking time: 15 minutes
500 g (1 lb) tamarind pods
3½ cups water
4 cups sugar

Clean and wash the tamarind pods. Place them in a large bowl, add the water and soak overnight. Drain the liquid into another bowl and reserve.

Extract the pulp from the pods by pressing them with a wooden spoon through a fine strainer.

Strain the extracted pulp back into the reserved liquid. Mix together, strain and squeeze through cheesecloth into a saucepan. Add the sugar.

Slowly bring the mixture to the boil, stirring constantly. Lower the heat and simmer until the syrup thickens. Remove from the heat, cool slightly and pour into bottles.

When completely cool, seal with airtight lids.

Dilute 2 tablespoons of this syrup in a glass of iced water to make a cordial drink.

Variation:
To use this syrup for flavouring stews, stuffed vegetables and other foods, reduce the amount of sugar to 2 cups.

INDEX

Arabic names are printed in italics,
chapter headings in capitals.